COPING SKILLS
FOR TEENS

---

*A Step-By-Step Guide to Emotional Mastery:
Overcome Anxiety and Cultivate a Deep
Understanding of Self*

B.B. Glynn

TABLE OF CONTENTS

Introduction...1

Chapter 1: *Understanding the Terrain* 4

   Deciphering Teenage Emotions...4

   The Intricacies of Anxiety 9

   Brain Basics: How Teens Think and Feel........................16

   External Factors and Their Emotional Impact.................20

Chapter 2: *Step 1 –Recognizing and Labelling Emotions* 23

   The Power of Naming.. 23

   Understanding the Emotional Spectrum 27

   The Role of Body Language... 31

   Emotions and Decision Making 37

   Emotion Wheel Exploration 42

Chapter 3: *Step 2 – Mindful Presence* 44

   The Magic of Mindfulness.. 45

   Embracing the Present Moment 51

   Cultivating a Mindful Environment 67

Chapter 4: *Step 3 – Navigating Emotional Triggers*........................... 88

   Mapping Your Emotional Triggers....................................89

   Strategies for Diffusing Triggers 102

   The Role of Memory in Triggers 105

   Empowering Through Education......................................106

Chapter 5: *Step 4 - Hassle-Free Techniques to Combat Anxiety* 109

Breathing Through the Stress... 110

Grounding Oneself in the Present 113

Harnessing Positive Distractions 114

Building a Toolkit for Anxiety 115

Chapter 6: *Step 5 - Conversations with Self* 117

Challenging the Inner Critic..118

Affirmations for Self-Understanding..119

The Role of Self-Reflection... 120

Establishing a Dialogue with the Future Self.......................................121

Chapter 7: *Cultivating Deep Self-Understanding*............................ 125

Embracing Self-Compassion 126

Reflecting on Growth and Resilience 128

Developing Intuition and Inner Wisdom..128

Reconnecting with Core Values 130

Chapter 8: *The Journey Continues* 132

A Lifelong Commitment to Self-Understanding 133

Seeking External Guidance and Wisdom...135

Creating an Environment of Growth..136

Revisiting and Renewing Commitments...139

Conclusion 141

References 142

INTRODUCTION

"It takes courage to grow up and become who you really are."

—E. E. Cummings

Teenagers go through a rollercoaster of emotions, and being able to communicate with family members or friends might be challenging. It's essential to address every feeling, understand the emotions behind it, and learn how to positively deal with a situation to blossom into a strong and responsible individual.

Ignoring problems during your teen years will stagnate growth and prevent you from maturing and building trust, which is the base of all relationships. From anger to depression to constantly feeling that no one understands you, it's common for teenagers to feel they have the weight of the world on their shoulders.

Whether you're socially awkward, anxious, tend to make questionable decisions, or are simply low on energy, this book will help you navigate through every situation in life. Don't let the problem get the better of you. Learning how to cope with your emotions opens doors to more opportunities and helps you grow. This also enables you to establish strong relationships with the people that matter.

Let's look at an example. A young boy named Ethan was excited about asking Tess to prom. He was confident and decided to ask her in the hallway. The next day, Ethan woke up all excited. He knew today was going to be the best day of his life. He couldn't focus on his studies the entire day.

The moment had finally arrived. He saw Tess standing by her locker after school. He gathered the courage and walked up to her. Tess turned around and gave him a friendly smile. This encouraged Ethan, and he asked her to prom. She politely told him she had already said yes to Craig. Ethan's heart broke. He didn't know how to handle this situation. He felt like his world had come crashing down.

Ethan rushed home and locked himself in his room. He refused to come down for lunch and continued crying. How could this happen to me? What should I do next? Will it be awkward seeing Tess or Craig at school? These questions haunted Ethan, and he just didn't know where to find the answers.

I'm sure he would have loved a guide that would answer all teens' questions during their growing years. This is where this guide comes in, and it's different from other self-help guides. It will not preach what you should and shouldn't do. I've crafted this guide with step-by-step details on handling those difficult teen years. This guide will help transform your struggles and pain into manageable situations.

By the end of the book, I assure you that you will have more clarity about different life situations and less chaos—be it at home or school. You will learn how to completely control different situations in your life. You will learn how to manage your emotional reactions and become a better, more mature person.

CHAPTER 1:

Understanding the Terrain

"I think you go through a period as a teenager of being quite cool and unaffected by things."

—Miranda Otto

Trying to navigate teen years is a never-ending maze. One question leads to another, and it feels like there are a million puzzles to solve every step of the way. While most teens love diving head-first into every difficult situation, that's not ideal. Start by understanding what's happening around you. Learn how your emotions develop and how external factors shape them.

Deciphering Teenage Emotions

The brain is still in development during the teen years. Apart from the physical changes, it's a phase where one discovers and explores various facets of their behavior. The gray matter in the brain slowly starts developing, and with it comes reasoning and problem-solving.

This phase also calls for patience from parents. Most parents are intolerant of their child's behavior. Sometimes, there's no effort to understand the hormonal changes a teen is going through. This adds to the confusion, and most teens become vulnerable to risks.

While parents are often advised to communicate clearly and regularly with their teen children, the effort should go both ways. Children should also make an effort to speak up and explain what's happening. As mentioned earlier, a lot changes during the teen years. Apart from the physical and psychological changes, you also begin discovering ways to control your emotions. Let's look at the emotional aspect and how it affects you.

Emotional Development During Teenage Years

As mentioned above, the teen years are when everything starts feeling different. You begin getting intense feelings and emotions. Most of the time, your mood will be unpredictable. This is because your brain is still learning to express and control emotions. Most of you may try to suppress these intense bursts of feelings because you don't want to look weak or vulnerable in front of your family or friends.

You will also begin understanding what others are feeling. This is called "empathy." You will start reading body language and facial cues; however, there will be times you will misread these. Take your time, and don't rush into making assumptions. It is also advisable to speak with someone about the things you're going through. No one can handle this development phase alone.

Another aspect that will start getting affected is your self-esteem. The most significant contributor to this is your physical changes. Comparisons to others' bodies will begin, and you will start questioning every change you're undergoing. This, again, calls for an open conversation with an adult. Speak with them and explain what you're going through. It may not be that simple, owing to the emotional outburst in your head, but it's worth trying.

Role of Hormones, Societal Pressures, and Personal Growth

Hormonal fluctuations are one of the most significant changes you will undergo. Due to the changes brought on by puberty, your sexual development and physical growth will see a substantial increase. Your emotions and feelings will get stronger. Some even undergo mood swings or weight gain owing to the growth spurt. These changes will also see you taking more risks due to strong impulses.

Hormonal changes affect your mind and body, apart from your behavior. If you're feeling such strong urges, speaking with your parents, teachers, coaches, and even your elder siblings is always advisable. You need to learn how to control your emotions and overcome these challenges. Now, let's look at the stages of puberty so you understand what you're going through and what to expect.

Stage 1

This stage begins around seven or eight in girls and around nine or 10 in males. During this stage, your brain will signal your body to start producing sex hormones and you will start seeing a few physical changes.

Stage 2

This stage begins between nine and 11 in girls and at age 11 in males. This stage will see even more physical changes.

Stage 3

Stage 3 begins around the age of 12 in females and around the age of 11 in males. This stage includes growth spurts and noticeable physical changes. For example, the average height girls grow in a year is about 2.4 inches. Once stage 3 begins, they grow about 3.1 inches a year. Post menarche (onset of the menstrual cycle), their growth rate slows down and they grow between 2-3 inches a year. Similarly, boys grow about 3.5 inches a year before spermache (sperm in seminal fluid). The growth spurt for boys lasts longer than girls.

Stage 4

This stage begins around 13 in females and 14 in males. This is the most intense point of puberty. During this stage, boys start developing a deeper voice and females usually get their first period (this can happen earlier in some females).

Stage 5

This stage begins around the age of 15 for males and females. This is the final stage of puberty. In most cases, this signals the end of physical development.

How the Evolving Teenage Brain Influences Emotional Processing

Now, let's talk about your brain. No matter how well you perform academically, handling emotions and excelling at handling them are different ballgames. Your rational part of the brain isn't developed yet and won't be until you reach about 25. Research shows that adults think and make decisions using their prefrontal cortex. This is the rational part of the brain. You, on the other hand, use your amygdala to make decisions. This is the emotional part of your brain.

While the connection between the emotional and decision-making parts of the brain is fully developed in adults, it's still a work in progress for teens. Most often, this development does not happen at the same rate. Therefore, you may sometimes feel emotionally overwhelmed and unaware of your thoughts. This is because you're feeling more than you're thinking at this stage.

It's normal to see teens go into their shells when emotions get the better of them. However, if you feel you cannot snap out of this, speak to an adult, preferably a parent or counselor. In most cases, teens usually make impulsive decisions. It's better to get help and express your feelings rather than suppressing them.

The Role of Societal Norms and Peer Pressure in Shaping Emotional Responses

Your peers also play a massive role in how you respond to emotions. Most teenagers succumb to peer pressure and do something they don't usually do. This means there will be times you choose to suppress your feelings just so your friends don't see you as an outcast and you feel accepted. It's more about pleasing peers than discovering the changes within you.

If you feel your peers are pressuring you into doing something you don't want to do, make sure you report it. The easiest thing to do is speak to your parents. If they aren't available, talk to your siblings or a relative. Be happy with your choices, and don't let others influence your development.

Similarly, societal pressure plays a huge role in influencing your behavior. You may be compelled to behave in a certain manner in front of others because that's more "acceptable." Learn to be happy with your choices and stick with them, no matter what. I know it's easier said than done, but there's no reward without a bit of effort.

The Intricacies of Anxiety

Being anxious is only normal, irrespective of how old you are. It can stress your body out and cause a sudden hormonal surge, making you act in a particular way. There are various reasons why a person can be anxious. It could be interacting with someone new, taking a test, or speaking in class. This section will delve into the details of understanding your anxiety and dealing with it.

The Science Behind Anxiety

The reason one gets anxious is because of an imbalance between the inhibitory parts of the brain and your emotions. An anxious person has two responses: Fight or flight. This is because anxiety prepares your body to fight danger or perceivable danger, even if it doesn't exist in some situations.

Many teens confuse anxiety with fear. You should know that stimuli trigger your fears. So, when the stimulus disappears, fear goes along with it. On the other hand, anxiety continues to stay and even grow in some situations.

Most teens go through something like generalized anxiety disorder. This is an overwhelming feeling of worry, contemplating something bad even if it will never happen. When you're anxious, you start experiencing hypersensitivity, which makes your thoughts go out of control, often imagining the worst.

Recognizing the Signs and Symptoms

Every individual experiences anxiety differently. I've listed down various symptoms you may or may not experience, along with certain other symptoms that might not be recognized yet.

Effects on Your Body

Anxious people often feel the following symptoms:

- Churning in their stomach
- Dizziness or lightheadedness
- Needles and pins all over the body
- The inability to stay still and constant restlessness
- Backaches, headaches, and other forms of pain

- Rapid breathing
- Irregular heartbeat or constant thumping in your chest
- Hot flushes or cold sweats
- Difficulty in sleeping
- Teeth grinding at night
- Nausea
- Constipation or diarrhea
- Frequent urination
- Panic attacks

Effects on Your Mind

When it comes to the mind, these are symptoms to look out for:

- Feeling nervous, tense, or unable to relax
- Feeling of awfulness where you fear the worst and dread it happening
- Feeling that things are going too fast or too slow
- Believing that others can see your stress
- The nonstop worry cycle where you think that if you stop worrying, something terrible will happen
- Contemplation of a possible panic attack
- Constantly looking for reassurance from others and stressing that you've upset them or that they're angry with you
- A feeling that you're losing touch with reality
- Being in a low state of mind or slipping into depression
- Reliving all the bad experiences in your life

- Disassociating yourself from your mind or body and feeling like you're seeing yourself as an outsider
- The constant feeling of disconnection from the world

Certain studies state that people who constantly go through anxiety may develop physical health problems, such as heart problems, diabetes, or stomach ulcers. While there isn't enough evidence to support the facts, these conditions are still seen in people who are more anxious. It's also correlated since people who have a physical illness or disability tend to get more anxious or stressed, so it's a vicious circle that goes around. If your physical condition can be treated, it can control the anxiety.

Long-Term Effects of Anxiety

Anxiety isn't something you can get over quickly. It would help if you learned how to deal with and control it. During this period, most people with anxiety will find it difficult to groom themselves regularly or practice essential cleanliness, be able to attend school/college regularly, build and maintain relationships, explore or try new things, and enjoy a relaxing day. People with severe anxiety find it difficult to focus on their studies and perform well academically. They also struggle to socialize and spend time with friends or family.

Types of Anxiety Disorders in Teens

There are various types of anxiety disorders. This section will look at what they're all about.

Generalized Anxiety Disorder

As mentioned above, this is the most common disorder seen in teens. It's an overwhelming feeling of worry, stress, and tension without an actual reason.

Panic Disorder

This is a sudden outburst of intense fear you experience, which then causes a panic attack. This disorder will cause you to break into a sweat, where your heart beats uncontrollably, and you may believe you're having a heart attack because of the palpitations. You may also experience a choking sensation and difficulty breathing.

Social Anxiety Disorder

This disorder is often called "social phobia" since it causes you to worry and become self-conscious whenever you encounter a social situation. It makes you worry about what people think of you and whether you'll be ridiculed, embarrassed, or judged.

Specific Phobias

This intense fear sets in when you believe you're put in a situation you're afraid of, such as being exposed to flying or heights. It may cause a variety of feelings, including imagining the worst and becoming irritable.

Agoraphobia

This is the feeling of being stuck in a situation and unable to escape during an emergency. This fear is most commonly seen when you board a flight, are in a crowded place, or are traveling by public transport.

Separation Anxiety

While it's most commonly seen in children, they're not the only ones anxious when separated from their loved ones. If you suffer from separation anxiety when somebody close to you isn't in front of you, you become anxious and begin imagining something terrible happening to them.

Selective Mutism

This subtype of social anxiety is most commonly seen in younger children. Although verbal in front of their family, they will not speak when at school or in public.

Medication-Induced Anxiety Disorder

Abusing certain drugs or withdrawals from them can trigger certain anxious feelings, including an irregular heartbeat, cold sweats, and panic.

The Link Between Anxiety and Other Mental Health Issues

The link between anxiety and other mental health issues is quite common. When you understand its existence, it becomes easy to treat the condition.

Phobia and depression

Phobias cause anxiety and can often blur the lines between reality and the imaginary world. This causes irritability, confusion, and sometimes hallucinations. Severe cases can turn into a psychotic illness called "schizophrenia." This condition often leaves people feeling sad, lonely, and often unable to express themselves. Although they are two completely different mental disorders, there's a high possibility that people with schizophrenia will suffer from depression.

Eating Disorder

An anxiety disorder can often lead to an eating disorder where people find solace in food. According to the National Institute of Mental Health, an eating disorder is partially caused by depression, and the treatment course may include using antidepressants to make the person feel better.

An eating disorder doesn't always mean overindulgence of food. It sometimes results in complete aversion, causing anorexia, a common condition in teenage girls. The longer it's ignored, the more harmful it can get. If you're anxious about how you look or someone has body-shamed you, it can result in this disorder. You start to restrict how much you eat and even abuse the use of laxatives or enemas and force yourself to throw up, causing severe nutritional deficiencies in the body. People with an eating disorder often feel sad or low, which causes depression.

Substance Abuse

Individuals who abuse drugs, alcohol, or tobacco are at high risk of depression. While people believe that the use of substances can help deal with anxiety, it's the opposite. Substance abuse often leads to people feeling lower than ever. It develops a sense of frustration and takes a toll on their physical life. Individuals with social anxiety often believe that certain substances can help them be more social, but it only makes them feel more antisocial than ever.

Abruptly stopping the use of certain substances can cause withdrawal, which increases anxiety and may make a person feel like relapsing. Substance abuse is often treated with detoxes and antidepressants to uplift a person's mood and help them.

Brain Basics: How Teens Think and Feel

There are many significant changes that occur in the brain during adolescence. Understanding these changes is vital for healthy growth and development. This section will look at the teen brain and how it functions.

Brain Areas in Focus: The Prefrontal Cortex, Amygdala, and Their Roles in Emotion

The prefrontal cortex is like the central processing unit in your brain that helps manage your thoughts and emotions. The primary function of the prefrontal cortex is to regulate the amygdala and control the emotional stress response.

The amygdala is the structure of the brain that detects stress. It, in turn, sends a message to the hypothalamus–pituitary–adrenal (HPA) on how to respond. The HPA is a messenger system in the brain. It signals how the various organs in your body will react to stress by going into survival mode.

The Reward-Seeking Teen: How the Brain's Pathways Contribute To Emotional Highs and Lows

A healthy brain combines the right environmental influence, the thought process, how you react to your thoughts, how you feel about it, and how you control emotions. Time-management is akin to healthy brain development. Getting involved in various activities that combine intellectual and extracurricular activities in the proper doses can help shape your brain better.

A bright atmosphere at home is also essential for proper brain development. This can be incorporated by positive behavior encouragement, adequate sleep, and good thinking skills.

During the development stage, it's common for teens to want to be involved in high-risk activities, make impulsive decisions, and express strong emotions. This may be overwhelming to deal with, but positive enforcement and seeking the guidance of elders is an intelligent way to allow your brain to develop better and control anxiety.

While risks are acceptable, they should be calculated and under the guidance of the right people. Risks should only be taken to impress and fulfill you, not anyone else. You should also respect the trust your parents put in you while allowing you to take the risk.

Finding an expressive outlet is an excellent way to develop your brain. Music, sports, and writing are amazing ways to express yourself and learn something. You must also be aware that every action has a potential consequence. A negative action will have a negative outcome and vice versa. Always remind yourself that negative is unhealthy and positive is healthy, so you train your brain to focus on positive activities.

Family routines help form structure, so ask your family to create a routine that involves you contributing towards the house, even if just in small ways. This will teach you to be a team player. Respect the boundaries your elders set for you because while you may not understand them, they reinforce healthy qualities that will benefit you throughout your life. Also, find a strong role model for yourself and learn how to incorporate healthy habits so you can move forward in the right direction.

One of the biggest mistakes teens make is not communicating with their parents. They were once young and went through similar situations. The closer you are to them and the more open you choose to be, the less anxious you will get.

The Adaptability of the Teen Brain and the Chance for Positive Change

A teen brain is complicated. It's no longer a child's brain and hasn't fully developed into an adult brain either. You can consider it a half-baked brain with its timer set, and it must be set at the right emotional temperature for it to bake correctly.

The emotions in your brain are driven by the limbic system, and this intensifies during puberty. Since the prefrontal cortex isn't fully developed, there's often an overflow of emotions, which makes teens highly adaptable and also more eager to take a risk.

Since puberty is now arriving earlier than ever, the mismatch in the brain is a lot higher, which causes a rush of emotions. This causes you to act out. The term "teen brain" is often considered an oxymoron. This is where the risky, aggressive outbursts that parents dread set in.

Understanding the evolution of the teen brain that's moving towards an adult one helps control emotions. Simple environmental and communication modifications help make these changes easier to deal with and reduce the risk of anxiety.

The Influence of Modern Technology on the Teenage Brain and Emotions

A recent study revealed that teens who spend a lot of time on social media impact their brain development. They tend to have a different association with social rewards and punishment. While there isn't enough data to support these facts, it's believed that the amygdala is preferentially affected by constantly checking social media. It also makes the procession of negative or positive emotions difficult.

Social media has become sort of an addiction for teens, and because it is so rampant in today's teens, it isn't easy to disassociate with it. This is the first generation that has seen social media since birth. While social media does have adverse effects, it also has positive effects. The key is to balance it right.

External Factors and Their Emotional Impact

Being a teenager isn't easy. You need to put up with various stressful situations regularly, which could result in anxiety. Whether it's not being able to meet school demands or frustration with your peers, certain teenagers have more stress than others. This results in various forms of anxiety. Dealing with these situations can help control anxiety and promote better brain development.

Academic Pressures: The Stress of School, Grades, and Future Planning

The constant need to perform better than your peers can lead to academic pressure, which results in anxiety. Whether you're obsessed with grades or feel extremely competitive to do better than others, it can cause sleep difficulties, social isolation, and even substance abuse when you overthink.

Accepting who you are and being happy with the outcome, knowing you did everything in your power to perform well, is key. Surround yourself with the right people who don't pressurize you or make you feel less worthy of yourself.

Family Dynamics and Emotional Health: How Family Relationships Contribute to or Alleviate Emotional Struggles

I've already mentioned the importance of healthy communication with your family and why it's key for healthy brain development. If you haven't been able to have open and healthy communication with your family, you should begin right away. If you feel your parents aren't comfortable having a conversation with you, initiate a conversation and talk about your needs and how they can support you.

If you're in an unfortunate situation where you don't have supportive family members, look for an older person who can provide you with the proper support. This could be a teacher or a counselor at school, relatives, or even your friends' parents. If your parents tend to say something you dislike or feel is hurtful, you must let them know. Remember, they're human, too, and the only way you can have a healthy relationship with them is by honestly sharing how you feel with each other.

The Challenges of Digital Socialization: Navigating Online Interactions and Their Emotional Implications

Peer acceptance has become one of the most critical factors for teens today. Appearance matters more than the actual nature of a person. One wrong comment on your social media can pull your entire world down, mainly because it's not just you who reads the comment but your entire digital social circle.

Cyberbullying has become more prominent because it's easier to hide behind the screen and say mean things to others. Although this is rampant, you should remember you're always in control of what you want to expose yourself to. Simply blocking mean people and learning how not to let others affect your mental well-being is something you've got to teach yourself. You should also remember it's important you shouldn't do what you wouldn't want done to you.

Seeking Identity in a Diverse World: The Journey of Self-Discovery and Its Challenges

No two people are the same. Whether you're of a different skin tone or physical size or identify as a different gender, you must remember that you won't always fit in. Sometimes, standing out can be a good thing.

Learning to embrace your uniqueness is challenging, but once you do it, you'll be able to navigate the world, whether you face curiosity, compassion, or criticism. External pressures or an internal conflict may often disconnect you from who you really are. Whether you're fully aware or confused, talking to the right people can help. Start with family and close friends, and even consider therapy if needed.

Dealing with your emotions is a lot to take in. Now that you've understood the role emotions play and how you can identify them, it's time to recognize these emotions so you can learn how to control and convert your weaknesses into strengths.

The first stage to successfully controlling your emotions is to identify them. The next chapter will help you recognize and label your feelings. This will help you manage them better in different scenarios. Being a teenager is overwhelming, but learning to deal with your emotions enables you to successfully navigate life's challenges. It also helps develop your brain better.

CHAPTER 2:

Step 1 -Recognizing and Labelling Emotions

N ow that you clearly understand what different emotions mean, it's time to understand how to manage them in various situations. Imagine being in a situation where you feel an overflow of emotions but don't really understand what you're going through. The feeling is similar to when you're handed a box of crayons with no labels. It's confusing, frustrating, and annoying not knowing how to correctly label your emotions. It's time to decipher the emotional complexity in your life and figure out what's important and what's not. Let's begin an imperative journey towards identifying, labeling, and controlling emotions.

The Power of Naming

Research states that identifying and labeling negative emotions when you experience them can help reduce their intensity and duration. This technique is called effective labeling, a straightforward process involving expressing your feelings in words. For example, saying you're angry, upset, or stressed. This section will look at how labeling emotions can help you better control your feelings and not let them get the better of you.

How Labeling Emotions Can Reduce Their Intensity

When you don't know what you're experiencing, it creates chaos and uncertainty, and you're often overwhelmed by the feeling. Unless you know what you're dealing with, you can't get to the source of it. When you identify negative emotions, it helps reduce the intensity of the emotion. Similarly, when you experience positive emotions, it helps increase their intensity and duration. So, how does labeling an emotion reduce negative emotions and magnify positive emotions?

Labeling emotions helps you self-reflect on them. This helps you get better control over the situation and deal with it better. Labeling an emotion is easy. All you need to do is express yourself verbally, silently or loudly. You can simply say, "I am upset right now," or "I am happy." To further reduce the strength of negative emotion, you can add a psychological distance between the emotion by saying something like, "I notice that I am upset." According to Acceptance and Commitment Therapy (ACT), adding the prefix "I notice that..." helps create further distance between your emotions and helps diminish them.

Aiding Emotional Regulation: The Role of Precise Language in Managing Our Emotions Effectively

Regulation is your ability to manage behavior and how you react to others around you. This includes reacting to strong emotions, such as excitement, frustration, and anger. Emotional regulation is the ability to calm down after you're excited or upset. It helps you focus on the task at hand and control your impulses. You begin behaving in ways that help you get along with others.

Why Is It Important?

With self-regulation, you begin learning better. You learn better at school because it allows you to listen and focus in the classroom. You also begin self-regulation in socially acceptable ways. It enables you to control your impulses.

Self-regulation also allows you to make more friends. This is because you begin expressing emotions appropriately, sharing, and taking turns. You also become more independent. You learn to control your behavior and react in challenging situations with less guidance.

Developing Self-Regulation

You can develop self-regulation by watching the elders around you. The process begins in your childhood when you seek comfort through your actions. For example, some babies suck their fingers or blankets. Some toddlers are overwhelmed by emotions, which can be seen as temper tantrums if they see something they want.

By the time kids are in middle school, they begin to understand their emotions and control them slightly better. Empathy develops, and they start looking at things from others' perspectives. Teens, like you, are usually better at controlling emotions. You learn how to behave in a socially acceptable manner. You also begin caring about others' feelings and try to be more sensitive. This level of self-regulation will serve you well during your adult years.

Avoiding Emotional Suppression: The Importance of Acknowledging, Not Avoiding, Our Feelings

Today, there are emotional challenges around every corner. Teens are pressured to do well at school, keep up with their peers, and avoid FOMO (fear of missing out). All this can bring out strong emotions that may seem impossible to control.

However, the one problem with today's society is children are taught how to suppress their emotions rather than work with them. There are many ways of suppressing emotions, be it through prescription drugs, alcohol, etc. It's easy to take this path and ignore emotions completely. However, to what extent? Statements like 'mind over matter,' 'suck it up,' and 'learn to live with it,' exemplify how society has trained young brains since childhood. Suppressing emotions not only affects you mentally, but it also affects your physical health. A classic example is pressing down on the gas and brakes simultaneously. You will get nowhere, and a lot of pressure will build up.

Almost every emotion demands a physical reaction. However, since the brain has been trained to restrict such things, people use tactics like deep breathing and muscle contraction. This gives rise to depression and anxiety. Emotions shouldn't be ignored. While they may seem overwhelming initially, expressing them with the proper regulation is important.

It's important not to ignore your emotions so they don't affect you. Emotions play an important role in maintaining your physical and mental well-being. Don't avoid painful emotions because of what you're taught to do. If you want to develop a healthy mindset, you need to experience your emotions and work with them. This will help you function and feel better.

Understanding the Emotional Spectrum

Emotions affect almost everyone. This gives you all the more reason to understand them in the best way possible. While this is easier said than done, there are a few simple methods this section will speak about. One of the main methods is categorizing emotions. The main categorization is primary and secondary emotions. Let's learn more about them and how you can identify them.

Differentiating Between Primary and Secondary Emotions

Primary emotions are nothing but your initial reaction to certain events. Secondary emotions are the reactions you have to these reactions. While some believe that not all emotions can be categorized as primary or secondary, those that follow the Plutchik Model categorize primary emotions as trust, joy, anger, sadness, and disgust.

Let's take a few examples. Your journal was rejected. Your primary emotion will be discouragement; however, your secondary response will be anxiety. You've realized you need to redo the journal, and your primary emotion turned into a secondary emotion. Similarly, let's say your brother broke your favorite coffee mug. Your primary emotion would be anger, and you would yell at him. Your secondary emotion would be embarrassment at you yelling at him. Many people may also feel terror when they first hear the mug crashing. The well-being of their brother triggered a different primary emotion.

In these two scenarios, is your primary emotion justified? In the case of the journal, discouragement is probably justified. However, in the case of the mug breaking, is anger justified? Will it bring the mug back? Probably not. However, yelling at your brother will hurt him. Learning to categorize emotions will help you react better in such situations.

Journaling is one of the best ways to interpret emotions. Spend about 10 minutes each day to pen down the emotions you felt during the day. Then, note down your primary and secondary reactions to those situations. This could be anything like the frustration of waiting outside the bathroom when your sibling was using it or something your classmates said about you that made you react in a certain way. Come up with one word for each of the emotions. This will help you categorize it and also help you react better when something similar happens.

The Interconnectedness of Emotions

One of the critical determinants of mental health in teens is their connectedness to peers and family members. There is a direct relation between social connectedness and the use of social media. One of the best ways to understand emotions and their interconnectedness is to measure social media use and be open with family and peers. Teens should understand how social connectedness works and prioritize trust above all else. This helps increase connections and does not make one dependent on online interactions.

Social connectedness is a feeling of closeness and belonging. It consists of different domains and helps determine mental well-being. By being connected with peers and family, online bullying can be managed better, leading to fewer instances of depression and anxiety.

Triggers and Reactions: Identifying What Sparks Certain Emotions

Every teen goes through a range of emotions daily. This includes anger, disappointment, and frustration. These emotions are usually responses to events such as things happening at school, work, or in society. Your reaction to these events will also change based on your frame of mind.

Another thing that teens go through is emotional triggers. This includes experiences, memories, or specific events. These triggers spark an intense reaction, irrespective of your mood. Most emotional triggers are a result of post-traumatic stress disorder (PTSD). Knowing what triggers your emotional response and how to control it will help you maintain good emotional health.

Identifying Emotional Triggers

Triggers vary for each person. For some, it would remind them of unwanted actions or words; for others, it would trigger an uncomfortable or sad memory. Some common triggers include betrayal, disapproval, insecurity, and rejection.

The best way to recognize your triggers is to focus on your mind and body. Some common physical symptoms include an upset stomach, a racing heart, dizziness, and excess sweating of palms. When you begin noticing these signs, take a moment to consider what has happened. See the reaction it has invoked and analyze what you could do better. For example, you came home from school, completed your homework, cleaned your room, and arranged your clothes. Your parents come home from work and do not say anything. You feel your hard work is being ignored, and it's common to feel angry or frustrated in this situation. Common physical reactions to this situation include clenched jaws and a pounding heart.

Most teens would snap at their parents; however, it's best to understand why you feel the way you do. What made you feel frustrated or neglected? Did something similar happen in the past? In most cases, you would see a connection with something that's happened in the past. If you don't see an obvious connection, it's time to continue digging. This is where your journaling habits will come in handy. If you feel strong emotions, it's important to see what caused them rather than fighting them.

Shifts in Emotional States: Recognizing the Fluidity of Our Emotional Experiences

Many teens can label their emotions easily. While most can differentiate between disappointment and frustration, others may struggle to label them. Most teens only focus on whether they feel good or bad at any point. Studies have shown that those with better emotional differentiation have better mental health.

Transitioning from childhood to adolescence is a time of substantial change, emotionally and physically. Understanding how to manage your emotional experience and navigate this transition with ease is important. It will provide insights into your mental state and protect you from psychopathology.

The Role of Body Language

Effective communication is essential for success in both personal and professional relationships. While your words play a role in communication, your body language often has the strongest impact. Body language refers to the physical behaviors, expressions, and mannerisms you use to communicate without words, often on an instinctual rather than conscious level.

Whether you realize it or not, you constantly send and receive wordless signals when you interact with others. These nonverbal behaviors, such as posture, gestures, tone of voice, and eye contact, convey powerful messages. They can create a sense of ease, build trust, and attract others towards you. They can also confuse and undermine the message you are trying to convey. This section will explore the relationship between body language and emotions and how they interact.

Physical Signs of Emotions: How Our Body Reacts When We Feel Certain Ways

When you experience an emotion, it sets off a series of changes in your body, thoughts, and behaviors. Scientists have discovered that emotions have multiple components that contribute to our reactions.

One component of an emotional reaction is its effect on your physical state. For instance, when you feel fear or anger, your heart rate may increase, and your breathing may become faster. Similarly, sadness can bring tears to your eyes. Emotions can even trigger automatic movements in certain muscles. For example, happiness might lead to a smile, an excited voice tone, and a more upright posture; actions you may not even be aware of.

In addition to these physical changes, emotions also influence how you think. Studies have shown that people tend to recall and dwell on sad memories when they are sad. On the other hand, when people are happy, they typically remember and focus on positive memories. Moreover, emotions can shape your perception of the world around you. When you're scared, you become more vigilant, searching for potential dangers, while happy individuals tend to notice and appreciate pleasant things throughout their day.

The final piece of the emotional puzzle is the impact on your behaviors and desires. Different emotions can lead you to behave in ways that are consistent with the emotion you're experiencing. For instance, you may feel an urge to yell or engage in a physical confrontation when angry. Similarly, when scared, you might want to flee or seek safety. In contrast, sadness may make you want to isolate yourself and avoid social interaction.

Overall, emotions encompass a complex combination of bodily reactions, cognitive shifts in thinking, and behavioral inclinations, highlighting the intricate and interconnected nature of your emotional experiences.

Reading Others: Developing Empathy and Understanding Through Recognizing Non-Verbal Cues

Empathy is a complex trait that involves the ability to understand and share the emotions and perspectives of others. It allows you to empathize with others and take actions that can improve their well-being. By putting yourself in someone else's shoes, you can develop a sense of compassion and may be inspired to help them in any way you can. This not only helps alleviate their distress but can also provide a sense of fulfillment for you.

Empathy is not limited to those you know closely. It can extend to strangers as well. For instance, if you see someone feeling lonely and isolated at a social gathering, you might empathize with them and initiate a conversation to make them feel included and valued. Researchers have identified two main components of empathy: Affective and cognitive empathy.

Affective empathy refers to the ability to experience and share the emotions of others. For example, if your parents are feeling stressed or sad, you may unconsciously mirror those emotions and feel similarly. Likewise, if your friend is happy and enthusiastic, you might find yourself smiling or feeling uplifted by their positivity.

On the other hand, cognitive empathy involves the capacity to understand and interpret another person's mental state. It lets you gain insight into their thoughts, emotions, and perspectives. With cognitive empathy, you can recognize when someone is feeling angry, which allows you to predict how they might react to certain situations.

Additionally, you can identify when someone is feeling helpless, which helps you anticipate any potential outbursts they may have. These two components of empathy are associated with different neural networks in the brain, which means that it is possible to have high cognitive empathy but low emotional empathy and vice versa.

Feedback Loops: How Our Body's Responses Can Intensify or Diminish Our Emotional Experiences

How you feel, think, and behave are interconnected and influence one another in a continuous feedback loop. Your emotions can shape your thoughts and actions, while your thoughts and actions can also impact your emotions. This means that your experiences, beliefs, and behaviors are all interconnected, constantly influencing and being influenced by one another.

When you experience a particular emotion, it can lead to specific thoughts and behaviors that align with that emotion. Similarly, certain thoughts can trigger corresponding actions and emotions. Importantly, new actions can also act as catalysts for new thoughts and emotions.

The brain has a natural tendency to seek alignment between your emotions, thoughts, and actions. It strives to create harmony and coherence among these elements. This means that a strong signal from any of these components can significantly impact the others. The brain's inclination for alignment can either work in your favor or against you, depending on the quality of your emotions, thoughts, and actions.

If you do not consciously intervene in this feedback loop, it can control your life and dictate your experiences. However, you possess the capacity to transcend and overcome this cycle. You are more than just your emotions, thoughts, and actions. You have the power to become the master of these aspects of yourself.

When you allow your feelings to dictate your thoughts and actions, you surrender control to something external. It amounts to relinquishing your own free will and agency. When your emotions take the lead in the feedback loop, you are no longer in control of your own life.

To regain control and assert your free will, it is important to be aware of and actively intervene in this feedback loop. By developing self-awareness and consciously choosing your thoughts, emotions, and actions, you can break free from the automatic and reactive patterns that can keep you trapped in a cycle of unhappiness or unhelpful behaviors. Taking charge of your thoughts, emotions, and actions allows you to navigate life with intention and create positive change.

The Link Between Body and Mind: Understanding How Physical Sensations and Emotions Are Intertwined

When you experience stress, your body releases two hormones: Adrenaline and cortisol. These hormones are commonly known as stress hormones because they provide a temporary energy boost, often described as an adrenaline rush, to help you quickly respond to potentially dangerous situations.

However, it's possible to feel stressed even when there's no immediate danger to escape from. Releasing these stress hormones too frequently can negatively affect the body over the long term. Some of these effects include weakened immune response, digestive problems, and slower healing processes.

While the connection between stress and physical health is easier to comprehend, it may be more challenging to understand how your thoughts and beliefs can also impact your health.

Negative thinking patterns, such as always assuming the worst, jumping to conclusions, and engaging in self-criticism, can make it more difficult to cope with health problems. The constant presence of a negative inner voice can have serious consequences for your overall well-being, and breaking away from these harmful thought patterns can be a daunting task. This is where mind-body therapies can play a crucial role in promoting healing.

Mind-body therapies are techniques that focus on relaxation and mindfulness, aiming to address the connection between the body and the mind. These therapies utilize the body to influence the mind positively and vice versa. Examples of mind-body therapies include acupuncture, art therapy, cognitive-behavioral therapy (CBT), group therapy, and many others.

These therapies recognize the intricate connection between physical and mental well-being and offer practical tools to foster relaxation, self-awareness, and positive thinking. By actively engaging in mind-body therapies, individuals can find relief from stress, improve their overall health, and enhance their ability to cope with health challenges.

Emotions and Decision Making

Adolescence is a critical period for learning how to make sound decisions and effectively manage strong emotions. Developmentally, this stage of life is marked by significant changes that prepare individuals to confront these tasks head-on.

During adolescence, your cognitive abilities undergo substantial maturation. You become better equipped to consider the needs and perspectives of others, think in abstract terms, and analyze complex issues more effectively than when you were younger. These cognitive developments lay the foundation for developing important decision-making skills and establishing emotional intelligence.

Mastering decision-making and emotional management is a skill set that requires practice and real-life experiences. It is through these experiences that you have the opportunity to learn from your mistakes and grow. The ability to make good decisions and navigate complex emotions is not innate but is honed through proactive engagement with real-world situations. This section will look at emotions and how they influence your choices.

Impulse vs. Thought: How Different Emotions Can Influence Our Choices

Emotional development in adolescents is a complex and ongoing process that involves the gradual improvement of their ability to perceive, assess, and manage emotions. This development is driven by biological changes occurring in their bodies and minds and external factors such as their environment and the context in which they interact.

During adolescence, young people develop a heightened awareness of their own emotions and those of others. However, this perception may still be somewhat fragile and unstable. It takes time for adolescents to fully understand and navigate their emotions, as they are still learning how to interpret and respond to the various feelings they experience.

In many cases, adults may have certain expectations that adolescents should keep their emotions separate from their performance in school, work, and other activities. However, managing emotions in such a complex environment can be challenging for adolescents. They often deal with a range of emotions, from excitement and enthusiasm to stress and anxiety, which can impact their ability to perform optimally in various domains of their lives.

Each adolescent may have a different response to the process of emotional development. Some may embrace new challenges as they gain independence, feeling excited and motivated to take on new experiences. Others may require more support and guidance to build confidence and manage their emotions effectively. Adults and caregivers must recognize and respond to these individual differences, providing the necessary support and resources to help adolescents navigate their emotional development.

The Importance of Emotional Intelligence in Decision-Making

Emotional intelligence, often called EQ or EI, encompasses the ability to understand, use, and manage your emotions effectively. Just as a high IQ is associated with academic success, a high EQ indicates success in social and emotional situations. Developing and honing your EQ skills can help you build strong relationships, make sound decisions, and navigate challenging circumstances.

EQ can be thought of as a form of people-smartness. Understanding others and being able to relate to them is a valuable asset in various aspects of life. Research even suggests that EQ is more important than IQ when it comes to achieving success in school or the workplace.

While some individuals naturally possess strong EQ skills, others may need to actively work on improving them. The encouraging news is that everyone has the potential to enhance their emotional intelligence with the right knowledge and practice. Unlike IQ, which is relatively fixed, EQ can be cultivated and developed.

Improving emotional intelligence involves gaining insight into your emotions and the emotions of others. It requires the ability to identify, regulate, and express emotions appropriately, as well as to recognize and respond empathetically to the emotions of those around you. Developing self-awareness, self-management, social awareness, and relationship management skills are all important components of EQ growth.

The Dangers of Reactive Decisions

Reactive decision-making refers to making quick or immediate decisions in response to problems that have occurred. It is the opposite of proactive decision-making, which involves anticipating events and making rational decisions based on foresight.

In proactive decision-making, individuals focus on identifying potential risks or events that could impact an organization. They gather insights and information to make informed decisions to help prevent or mitigate these potential problems. This strategic and forward-thinking approach aims to minimize the need for reactive decision-making.

On the other hand, reactive decision-making is a response to problems that have already occurred. These decisions are often made under pressure and without much time for careful consideration. Reactive decision-making is inevitable because the future cannot be fully predicted, and unforeseen problems can arise despite precautionary measures.

Studies have shown that the brains of adolescents work differently from those of adults when it comes to decision-making and problem-solving. The emotional and reactive amygdala plays a more significant role in teenagers, while the logical and thoughtful frontal cortex is less dominant. This difference in brain development makes adolescents more prone to acting on impulse, misinterpreting social cues and emotions, and engaging in risky behavior.

Furthermore, exposure to drugs and alcohol during the teenage years can impact brain development and further hinder rational decision-making. This can contribute to accidents, fights, and other risky behaviors.

Identifying and Overcoming Biases That Are Influenced by Our Emotional State

Biases and prejudices develop since childhood. Children form assumptions based on their experiences. These biases can also stem from influences such as parents, education systems, cultural institutions, and popular media like books, movies, and television shows. Over time, these unconscious biases can become deeply ingrained and go unnoticed.

Unconscious biases come in various forms. One common type of bias is how individuals perceive their thought processes and reasoning abilities. Examples include confirmation bias, where people selectively focus on information that confirms their attitudes, and affirmation bias, which involves emphasizing negative qualities in individuals that align with one's preconceived notions.

Other biases are directly connected to how people look. These biases often rely on stereotypes and can lead to discriminatory practices, such as ageism, racism, and beauty bias. This means people may be treated unfairly or differently based on race, age, or physical appearance.

Furthermore, some biases stem from how people behave. While these biases may not be as frequently discussed, they can still have significant effects. Holding biases based on personality traits can result in discrimination against individuals, as they may be unfairly judged or treated differently due to their behavior.

It is important to recognize unconscious biases and work towards overcoming them. This can involve questioning our assumptions, challenging stereotypes, and actively seeking diverse perspectives to promote fair and equitable treatment for all individuals, regardless of their backgrounds, appearances, or behaviors.

Emotion Wheel Exploration

The skill of identifying and understanding one's emotions is a component of emotional intelligence. Individuals with high emotional intelligence are able to accurately articulate their emotions, express themselves in detail, and possess a wide emotional vocabulary. Research suggests that expanding one's emotional vocabulary can enhance emotional regulation and overall emotional well-being.

The Emotion Wheel, developed by Gloria Willcox in 1982, is a valuable tool for individuals struggling to identify their emotions. It serves as a starting point to explore and distinguish various emotions.

There are several ways in which the Emotion Wheel can be utilized:

Self-reflection: It can be used to explore and recognize the emotions experienced at any given moment throughout the day. This allows you to gain insight into your emotional states and understand the factors influencing your feelings.

Daily emotional tracking: Utilizing the wheel, you can engage in daily self-reflection exercises to identify the range of emotions you have experienced over the course of the day. This awareness enables a deeper understanding of emotional patterns and triggers.

Exploring deeper emotions: The Emotion Wheel can assist in exploring complex and deeper emotional experiences. It provides a framework to delve into long-term emotions that may influence overall well-being or affect relationships.

However, it is important to acknowledge that you can experience a multitude of emotions simultaneously. The Emotion Wheel should not be used to avoid or replace "negative" emotions with "positive" ones. Instead, its purpose is to aid in identifying, accepting, and communicating one's emotional experience without judgment or suppression.

I hope this chapter helped you understand the importance of recognizing and labeling emotions. So, are you ready to fully understand and control them how you like? The next chapter is about mindfulness; the art of mastering your emotions. Recognizing them is only the first part. Be ready to truly understand each emotion and be present with it.

CHAPTER 3:

Step 2 - Mindful Presence

"If you want others to be happy, practice compassion.
If you want to be happy, practice compassion."

—*Dalai Lama*

The importance of mindfulness cannot be stated enough. This chapter will look at how mindfulness can help you improve your emotional health. You will get all the tools needed to help you experience your emotions and not be overwhelmed. This is the next big step towards understanding your emotions.

Imagine standing at the edge of a serene lake. Every thought you have creates a ripple in the water. The more frantic and numerous your thoughts, the choppier the water becomes. But if you could find a way to quiet those thoughts, even for a moment, the lake becomes calm, reflective, and clear. This is the power of mindful presence, and it's about to become your refuge amidst the storm of teenage emotions.

The Magic of Mindfulness

The concept of mindfulness is simple but profound. It implies that one's mind is wholly focused on the present moment, fully aware of what's happening, and consciously engaged in the physical space they inhabit. At first glance, this might seem uncomplicated. However, your mind tends to wander frequently, causing you to lose touch with the present moment. You become preoccupied with obsessive thoughts about the past or the future, leading to anxiety and stress.

Luckily, mindfulness can help you navigate these mental distractions. It serves as an anchor, bringing you back to reality, focusing your mind on the present moment, and fostering a connection with your body and surroundings. The best way to grasp the concept of mindfulness is by practicing it. Although it's difficult to explain in words, you can find various interpretations through books, websites, audio, and video resources.

This section aims to define mindfulness and its significance for teens like you. Through mindfulness, you can cultivate a heightened sense of awareness that brings mental clarity and emotional balance, leading to a sense of calm amidst the chaos of daily life. Being mindful helps you embrace the present moment and approach life's challenges with a sense of openness, curiosity, and balance, allowing you to live more fully and authentically.

Defining Mindfulness: What It Means To Be Truly Present

Mindfulness is a fundamental trait that every human possesses. It refers to the ability to be completely present in the current moment, fully aware of your surroundings and actions. It involves being conscious of your thoughts, feelings, and sensations without being consumed by them. When you are mindful, you are not easily swayed by external factors or overwhelmed by the circumstances happening around you.

It is important to note that mindfulness is not a skill that needs to be acquired or achieved. Instead, it is an intrinsic quality that exists within each person. Mindfulness does not require you to summon or manufacture it. Rather, you simply need to learn how to tap into it and access it effectively.

Mindfulness Practice Types

Although mindfulness is a natural trait that you possess, it can be nurtured and developed through various techniques. Below are a few examples of these techniques:

Seated, walking, standing, and moving meditation: These are traditional meditation practices where you intentionally bring your attention to the present moment. Seated meditation involves sitting comfortably and focusing on the breath or bodily sensations. Walking meditation involves slow and mindful walking. This allows you to pay attention to each step and the sensations in the body. Standing and moving meditations are similar, with an emphasis on being fully present in the body and the actions performed.

Short pauses: Mindfulness can also be cultivated by incorporating short pauses into your daily routines. These moments of stillness and awareness allow you to break free and bring your attention to the present moment. It can be as simple as taking a few conscious breaths before starting a task or pausing to appreciate your surroundings during a walk.

Integrating meditation with other activities: Mindfulness can be seamlessly integrated into other activities, such as yoga or sports. You can enhance your awareness and focus by bringing a meditative mindset to these activities. For example, in yoga, mindfulness can be applied by being fully present during each movement and noticing the sensations in the body. Similarly, in sports, mindfulness can be practiced by focusing clearly on the action without being distracted by past or future thoughts.

Benefits of Mindfulness Practice

While it is important not to fixate on the benefits of meditation during the practice itself, it is undeniable that mindfulness meditation offers numerous advantages. By engaging in the practice without seeking specific outcomes, you can truly immerse yourself in the present moment.

One of the key benefits of mindfulness is stress reduction. When you cultivate mindfulness, you can better observe your thoughts and emotions without judgment. This non-reactive awareness helps you navigate stressful situations with calmness and resilience, ultimately reducing the impact of stress on your mental and physical health.

Another advantage of mindfulness is enhanced performance. When you are fully present and engaged in the task at hand, your focus improves, allowing you to perform at your best. Directing your attention to the current moment can eliminate distractions and increase your productivity and effectiveness.

Furthermore, mindfulness meditation allows you to gain insight and awareness by observing the workings of your mind. This practice makes you more attuned to your thoughts, emotions, and behavior patterns. This increased self-awareness allows you to make conscious choices and respond skillfully and constructively to situations.

The Science Behind Mindfulness: How Mindfulness Practices Affect the Brain and Emotional Health

Mindfulness practice can bring about neuroplasticity, which means it can rewire your brain and transform your responses to acute stress. One area of the brain that is particularly influenced by mindfulness is the amygdala. The amygdala is an ancient part of the human brain that regulates fear, emotion, and stress responses.

Recent studies using MRI data have demonstrated that regular mindfulness practice can reduce the amygdala's grey matter volume. This reduction is thought to be associated with a dampening effect on the stress response. As a result, individuals who regularly engage in mindfulness may find themselves less reactive to stressors, as their amygdala becomes less likely to trigger the fight or flight response.

Another fascinating finding is the impact of mindfulness on the prefrontal cortex, which is responsible for higher-order cognitive functions such as problem-solving, planning, and emotional regulation. Research has shown that mindfulness can increase the prefrontal cortex's grey matter volume.

The Contrast With Autopilot: Recognizing When We Are Mindlessly Drifting Through Life

The human brain has two distinct systems that play different roles in our decision-making. The first system, known as the autopilot system, is responsible for your emotions and intuitions. These cognitive processes primarily take place in the amygdala. The autopilot system guides your daily habits, helping you make quick decisions, and reacts rapidly in life-or-death situations, triggering the fight or flight response.

While the autopilot system was essential for survival in the past when immediate threats were common, it is not well-suited for modern life. This system often treats minor stresses as if they were life-threatening, leading to a constant state of stress that harms your mental and physical well-being. Additionally, because intuitions and emotions can produce snap judgments that feel true, they sometimes lead you to behave in ways that are not in your best interest.

On the other hand, you have the intentional system, which represents your rational thinking. This system is centered around the prefrontal cortex. It enables you to engage in more complex mental activities, such as managing personal and social relationships, logical reasoning, and acquiring new thinking and behavior patterns.

Unlike the autopilot system, which functions without conscious effort, the intentional system requires deliberate activation and can be mentally tiring. However, with enough motivation and appropriate training, you can activate the intentional system when the autopilot system is prone to making costly mistakes.

The interplay between these two systems shapes your decision-making processes and influences your actions and behaviors. By understanding the strengths and limitations of each system, you can learn to balance and integrate them effectively. This leads to making more reasoned decisions and living morally fulfilling lives.

Immediate Benefits: The Peace and Clarity Gained From Moments of Mindful Presence

Practicing mindfulness profoundly impacts various aspects of your life, leading to improved well-being, physical health, and mental health. First and foremost, mindfulness enhances your overall well-being by cultivating attitudes that contribute to a satisfying life. By being fully present and aware of your experiences in the present moment, you can fully savor the pleasures of life as they occur. This ability to engage in activities with full attention and awareness enables you to derive greater enjoyment and fulfillment from your everyday experiences.

Additionally, mindfulness helps you develop a greater capacity to cope with adverse events, allowing you to navigate challenging situations with resilience and poise. By focusing on the present moment, mindfulness practice enables you to break free from excessive worrying about the future or dwelling on regrets from the past. This liberated mindset lets you let go of concerns about success and self-esteem, leading to a greater sense of overall contentment. Moreover, mindfulness enhances your ability to form meaningful and deep connections with others, fostering empathy, compassion, and enhanced relationship quality.

In addition to its impact on well-being, mindfulness has been shown to significantly benefit physical health. Scientific research has revealed that mindfulness techniques can help alleviate stress, a pervasive issue in modern society. By practicing mindfulness, you can effectively manage and reduce your stress levels, improving overall health. Furthermore, mindfulness has been found to have positive effects on heart health. It can help treat heart disease and lower blood pressure, reducing the risk of cardiovascular events. Additionally, mindfulness can alleviate chronic pain, improve sleep quality, and even alleviate gastrointestinal difficulties, highlighting the holistic impact of mindfulness on physical well-being.

Embracing the Present Moment

When it comes to staying present, it doesn't have to be the stereotypical image of meditation with sitting on a pillow, fingers pinched, eyes closed, and humming, unless that's what you prefer, in which case, go ahead. Meditation can be as simple as sitting still and looking out the window. It's about intentionally slowing down and blocking out distractions.

To practice being present, try setting aside three minutes twice a day. During these minutes, you can focus on naming three things you see, three things you feel, three things you hear, and three things you smell. This exercise helps train the brain to be fully in the present moment.

Not only does this practice help you stay present, but it also serves as an excellent way to reduce stress. By training yourself to be present, you become more aware of the benefits it brings. As you progress, you can gradually increase the time you spend on the exercise. It's important to grow to a point where you also pay attention to your emotions and sensations in the present moment.

The Challenge of 'Now': Overcoming the Distractions of Past Regrets and Future Anxieties

Living in the present moment allows you to fully experience life and let go of regrets and worries. Instead of constantly being consumed by thoughts of the past or future, you can focus on the here and now and find happiness and peace.

Firstly, it's important to understand that happiness is not dependent on external circumstances. By consciously focusing on happiness, regardless of what is happening around you, you can find true and lasting happiness.

Living in the present moment allows you to fully engage with and appreciate your current experiences. When you're constantly dwelling on the past or worrying about the future, you miss out on the richness and beauty of the present moment. There is so much to be grateful for and enjoy in the here and now, and by being fully present, you can savor every moment.

Moreover, when you live in the present moment, you release yourself from the burden of regrets and worries. Regrets about the past and worries about the future can weigh you down and prevent you from experiencing true joy. By letting go of these negative thoughts and redirecting your focus to the present, you free yourself from unnecessary suffering and open up to a sense of peace and contentment.

Past Regrets

It's common to get caught up in regrets about the past and worries about the future. You often find yourself dwelling on things you wish you had done differently or consumed by thoughts of what might happen in the days, weeks, or years to come. However, it's important to recognize that fixating on the past or the future doesn't serve you well. In fact, it only prevents you from fully experiencing and appreciating the present moment.

The key to releasing yourself from past regrets and future worries is to focus on living in the present moment. By consciously directing your attention to what you're doing right now, you can let go of the thoughts that pull you into the past or push you into the future. Instead, you can fully immerse yourself in the current experience, whether you're executing a simple task or an enjoyable activity.

When you choose to live in the present moment, you cultivate a mindset of acceptance and contentment. You acknowledge that what has already happened cannot be changed and that the future is uncertain. By embracing the present, you find peace and serenity. You don't allow regrets from the past to hold you back, nor do you allow worries about the future to consume you. Instead, you appreciate the beauty and significance of each moment as it unfolds.

Fear of the Future

It's natural to have concerns about the future, especially when faced with uncertainties and potential challenges. However, excessive worry and anxiety can affect your mental and emotional well-being. The good news is that there are practical steps you can take to alleviate your fears and live more fully in the present moment. Here are some strategies to consider:

1. **Identify your fears:** Take the time to write down and articulate the specific worries consuming your thoughts. By recognizing and acknowledging these fears, you can better understand the underlying causes and triggers.

2. **Challenge your thinking patterns:** Once you've identified your fears, critically evaluate the basis for these concerns. Ask yourself whether they are rooted in factual evidence or based on assumptions and anxieties. Often, we realize that our fears are exaggerated or irrational when we examine them objectively.

3. **Practice mindfulness:** Mindfulness intentionally focuses on the present moment without judgment. It involves bringing awareness to your thoughts, emotions, and bodily sensations. By cultivating mindfulness, you can redirect your attention away from anticipatory worries and immerse yourself in the present experience. Incorporate mindfulness techniques such as deep breathing, meditation, or body scans into your daily routine to help ground yourself in the present.

4. **Act towards your goals:** Instead of surrendering to worry and anxiety, channel your energy into constructive actions. Break down your goals into manageable steps and begin working

towards them. For instance, if you're worried about an up-coming exam, create a study plan and prepare early. Taking proactive steps allows you to regain a sense of control over your circumstances and reduces anxiety about the unknown.

Remember, shifting your focus to the present moment doesn't mean completely disregarding the importance of planning for the future or learning from the past. It's about finding a balance that enables you to acknowledge and address future concerns without allowing them to overshadow the present. By implementing strategies like mindfulness and taking proactive steps toward your goals, you can effectively manage your worries and live more fully in the present moment.

Sensory Mindfulness: Using Our Five Senses to Root Ourselves in the Present

Mindfulness is the practice of being fully present in the current moment, accepting your circumstances without judgment. To incorporate mindfulness into your daily life, it is important to become a keen observer. By engaging your five senses, sound, smell, sight, taste, and touch, you can connect with the present moment and enhance your experiences with the world around you. Taking the time to appreciate your senses can help you slow down and fully embrace each moment.

One way to practice mindfulness is through a sensory exercise called "5-4-3-2-1 grounding." The idea behind this exercise is that re-engaging with your senses can help calm racing thoughts and bring you back to the present moment. It is a simple practice that involves slowing down your breathing, lowering your heart rate, and allowing your body to relax by reassuring you that everything is okay. It only takes a few minutes to complete, making it accessible for anyone to incorporate into their daily routine.

To begin, find a quiet space where you can be alone for around five minutes. You don't need any special equipment or materials for this exercise. Sit straight, resting your hands on your thighs, and ensure you are comfortable. Take a deep breath, inhaling slowly and deeply. Now, follow these steps.

Sound

As you continue to take slow, deep breaths, begin to focus on the sounds around you. Allow yourself to become aware of the auditory sensations without judging or categorizing them as positive or negative. Simply notice the sounds that you can hear in your environment. This may include traffic noises, conversations, music, or other sounds that catch your attention.

As you spend more time in this exercise, you will notice that your awareness expands, and you become more attuned to the subtle sounds you may have overlooked. Initially, your attention may be drawn to the loudest or most intrusive sounds in your surroundings, but as you continue the exercise, you will hear even the faintest noises.

If your mind begins to wander or you struggle to focus on the sounds, gently bring your attention back to your breathing. Take a moment to regain control of your breath before refocusing on the auditory aspect of the exercise. By repeating this practice a few times, you will find it easier and more natural to quickly transition between focusing on your breath and the sounds around you.

Smell

After focusing on the sounds around you, shift your attention to your sense of smell. Begin to explore the different scents that are present in your environment. Take note of any aromas that catch your attention. Are there any lingering smells from recently cooked food? Can you detect the scents of the products you have used, such as your shampoo or fabric softener? If you have a window open, see if you can pick up any scents from the outside, such as the freshness of cut grass or the fumes from passing vehicles.

Again, it is important to approach this step without judgment or the need to categorize scents as good or bad. Simply observe the smells you can detect, and then allow them to pass by without attachment. If you have a weaker sense of smell, you can make this step easier by lighting a scented candle before your five-minute session, providing a consistent and noticeable fragrance to focus on.

Sight

If you closed your eyes during the previous steps, now is the time to open them and shift your focus to the sense of sight. Take a moment to look around your immediate surroundings and observe the finer details.

Engage with your sense of sight by noticing the colors, shapes, and patterns you see. Please pay attention to any dominant colors in the room and consider whether they give off a warm or cool feeling. Take note of missing elements or notable objects that catch your eye.

By grounding yourself in the present moment and bringing your attention to the visual aspect of your surroundings, you can experience a sense of embodiment and reduce the physical and mental symptoms that one often associates with anxiety. If you find it challenging to concentrate on the visual stimuli around you, you may choose to focus on specific objects. Some people find it helpful to select stones or gems with different textures, colors, and sizes. Alternatively, you can choose 5-10 different items that vary in texture, color, and size to focus on. This approach allows you to practice visual concentration and adaptability, enabling you to engage with your sense of sight in any environment.

Taste

The sense of taste may feel unusual to focus on during a mindfulness exercise, especially if you don't have anything to eat or drink. However, having something to sip or snack on can make this stage easier for some individuals, although it is not mandatory.

You can feel the sensations in your mouth if you don't have anything to consume. Notice how your tongue rests between your teeth and become aware of lingering tastes from a previous meal. Take a moment to observe how your saliva feels in your mouth.

In addition, you can try running your tongue over each tooth individually and explore the textures of your teeth. Move your tongue along the inside of your cheek and observe the different sensations it elicits.

If you have food or drink available, you can apply the concepts discussed in the previous steps to your tasting experience. Take the time to notice the various textures in what you are consuming. Are some parts smooth while others are rough? Do you detect any grooves or dips in the food? Pay attention to the distinctive flavors or ingredients you can identify. And after you swallow, observe whether any taste lingers in your mouth.

Touch

Moving on to the next step in the anxiety 5-4-3-2-1 grounding practice, you now shift your focus to the sense of touch. As you began this exercise, you placed both hands on your thighs. Check if your hands are still resting there. Observe what you can feel beneath your fingers. You may notice the warmth or coolness of your skin or perhaps feel the softness of your clothes against your hands.

However, it's important not to limit your attention solely to your hands. Expand your awareness of what is underneath your feet and the surface you are sitting on. Notice the various textures present in your surroundings. Pay attention to any areas of tension or relaxation in your body.

To complete the grounding practice, stand up from your seated position and purposefully touch one or two objects in the room. This step is particularly important, as it helps you continually train your attention on the present moment.

Throughout this five-minute meditation, it's common to encounter distracting thoughts. If this happens, gently bring your attention back to your senses. Don't be discouraged by these distractions; they are simply another engagement of a particular sense. Incorporate them into your practice and use them as an opportunity to enhance your awareness.

Coping Technique

When you experience anxiety, it can feel overwhelming and suffocating. The physical symptoms of anxiety, such as a racing heart, nervousness, and sweating, can make you believe that everyone around you is watching and judging you. Anxiety often brings a sense of impending doom, making you feel like everything is spiraling out of control.

Anxiety episodes can occur frequently in your daily life or may be triggered by particularly stressful days. These episodes are incredibly unpleasant and can significantly impact your overall well-being.

So, what should you do when you feel your anxiety intensifying? Use the above techniques. It helps to calm your body and your mind almost instantly. By grounding yourself, you can regain a sense of control and safety within yourself and your thoughts, even when anxiety tries to convince you otherwise. This exercise can give you the tools to cope with difficult emotions and anxiety, allowing you to navigate these challenging moments more resiliently.

Letting Go of Judgment: Approaching the Present With Acceptance, Not Evaluation

The mind is a constantly judging machine. It automatically filters, categorizes, and processes every experience you have. It classifies things as either "good," leading you to desire more and hold on to what you already have, or "bad," causing you to hide, resist, or run away. Everything else is considered "neutral" and often ignored.

There's nothing inherently wrong with this judgment process, as it is natural for the mind to do so. Sometimes, these judgments can be helpful. They can help you understand what brings you joy, energizes you, and gives your life purpose. They can also help you recognize what doesn't resonate with you and leaves you feeling drained. However, these judgments can become exhausting and controlling when they go unchecked. It takes a significant amount of energy to evaluate and judge every single experience you encounter.

When you are unaware of how your judgments shape your actions and reactions, you become a passive observer of your life. It is as if you are a marionette controlled by a puppeteer. Your conditioned judgments and automatic responses trap you in a cycle of reactivity. However, mindfulness offers a way to break free from this cycle through the practice of non-judgment.

Non-judgment involves letting go of the need to react immediately to the present moment. It means relinquishing the tendency to constantly grasp for more, resist what is happening, or ignore the experiences life presents to you. By releasing the desire to control or judge your experiences, you create space to fully embrace and engage with them. This allows you to rest in a state of mindful presence, where you are fully present and accepting of the present moment.

It is important to note that non-judgment does not imply that you will never experience judgments in your mind. The mind naturally tends to judge, and it is impossible to eradicate this tendency. Instead, non-judgment is about changing your relationship to these judgments. It is about recognizing them as temporary thoughts that arise and pass, rather than becoming consumed by them just because they surface in your mind. By observing and acknowledging these judgments without attaching to them, you can cultivate a sense of detachment and freedom from their influence.

Benefits of Non-Judgment

Practicing mindfulness means actively engaging with each experience as it unfolds. Being fully present and attentive gives you a sense of freedom and peace. This state of mindfulness brings numerous benefits, particularly when cultivating non-judgment.

- Non-judgment opens your eyes to the inherent beauty of life. When you label something "neutral," you may dismiss it as insignificant and unworthy of your attention. However, when you release judgment, you open yourself to the potential for wonder and awe in every aspect of life. Any activity, no matter how mundane, can become a source of joy and enrichment if you take the time to truly appreciate it.

- In addition, non-judgment helps free you from constantly pursuing more. Often, dissatisfaction arises when we believe that what we currently have is not enough. This judgment fuels a never-ending quest for money, achievements, or titles. By relinquishing this judgment, you can fully recognize and appreciate the countless positive qualities already present in your life.

- Furthermore, cultivating non-judgment contributes to a more peaceful state of mind. Your judgments are often the source of stress and dissatisfaction, particularly when perceiving the "bad" aspects of your life or anticipating negative outcomes. By letting go of the judgment that labels these experiences as negative, you can free yourself from the suffering caused by interpreting them in a negative light.

- Non-judgment also enhances your ability to see things clearly. When you react solely based on your judgments, you are limited to your subjective interpretation of reality. However, by releasing these judgments, you can perceive things as they truly are without the influence of conditioned thoughts and beliefs. This allows for a more accurate and unbiased understanding of the world around you.

The Art of Single-Tasking: Breaking Free From the Myth of Multitasking

In today's fast-paced world, multitasking is often considered valuable. However, research suggests that contrary to popular belief, focusing on one task at a time can actually be more effective. Single-tasking, or dedicating your full attention to a singular objective, offers numerous benefits that can enhance your performance, problem-solving abilities, and overall mental well-being.

When you engage in single-tasking, you can channel your energy and concentration into the task at hand. You create a sense of purpose and clarity by directing all your resources towards a specific goal. This focused mindset allows you to bring your best self to the task, increasing the likelihood of achieving a successful outcome.

Moreover, single-tasking provides an opportunity for improved performance. Committing your full attention to one task allows you to delve deeper into it and explore different angles and possibilities. This level of depth enables you to approach the task with greater creativity, innovation, and critical thinking. As a result, you are more likely to come up with unique solutions and produce higher-quality work.

In addition to enhancing performance, single-tasking can also reduce mental fatigue. Constantly switching between tasks and dividing your attention can be mentally draining, leading to decreased productivity and increased stress levels. Focusing on one task at a time allows your mind to fully engage and immerse itself. This immersion provides a sense of flow, where you are fully absorbed in the present moment and not overwhelmed by many distractions. As a result, mental fatigue is minimized, and you can sustain your energy and attention for longer periods.

Furthermore, single-tasking supports better problem-solving. When you focus on one task, you can give it your undivided attention and thoroughly explore different solutions and approaches. This depth of analysis allows for a more comprehensive understanding of the problem, leading to more effective and thoughtful solutions. In contrast, when multitasking, important details and connections may be overlooked, compromising the quality of your problem-solving process.

Avoiding Multitasking

Transitioning from multitasking to single-tasking requires a deliberate and conscious effort, but its advantages make it worthwhile. Here is a step-by-step process to help you break free from the multitasking trap and embrace single-tasking.

- **Prioritize Tasks:** Create a list of all the tasks you must accomplish for the day. Next, rank these tasks in order of importance, considering their impact on your overall goals. Identify the task that holds the most significance and should be prioritized.

- **Time Blocking:** Allocate dedicated time blocks for each task on your priority list. During these specified blocks, commit to focus exclusively on the assigned task. It is important to mute notifications and remove any potential distractions to ensure undivided attention.

- **Set Clear Goals:** Clearly define what success means for each task you undertake. Having a precise and measurable goal will help you stay motivated and engaged as you work towards achieving it.

- **Practice Mindfulness:** Engage in techniques such as deep breathing or meditation to center yourself before diving into a task. These mindfulness practices help enhance your concentration levels and reduce the urge to switch between tasks. You can optimize your focus and productivity by being fully present in the moment.

- **Eliminate Interruptions:** Inform your family members about your focused periods. Communicate when you will be engaged in a task and request that interruptions be minimized during those times. Set boundaries effectively and make your availability known to reduce distractions.

- **Celebrate Progress:** Once you finish a task, take a moment to acknowledge and celebrate your accomplishment. It can be as simple as a 60-second dance party or any other form of positive reinforcement that helps boost your motivation. Celebrating your progress creates a sense of fulfillment and satisfaction that encourages you to continue embracing the single-tasking approach.

It's easy to get caught up in the myth of multitasking, but it's important to remember that it is not always the most efficient approach to getting things done. When you invest yourself in a single task, you'll find that you complete each project at a higher level of quality and in less time than when you try to juggle several tasks simultaneously. Remember, your journey towards peak productivity begins with a single task.

Cultivating a Mindful Environment

Cultivating mindfulness is a practice that involves developing the ability to be fully present in the moment with a non-judgmental and accepting attitude. This practice can benefit individuals of all ages, including teenagers.

One of the primary benefits of mindfulness is the development of greater self-awareness. Practicing mindfulness makes you more attuned to your thoughts, feelings, and physical sensations. This increased self-awareness allows you to better understand yourself and your reaction to various situations. It enables you to recognize patterns of thought and behavior that may not serve you well and helps you make positive changes.

Another benefit of mindfulness is the enhanced ability to manage stress. Teenagers often face many stressful situations, whether academic pressure, social challenges, or personal issues. By cultivating mindfulness, teenagers can develop the skills to recognize and respond to stress in a healthy and constructive manner. They can learn to observe their stressors without becoming overwhelmed and choose more effective coping strategies.

There are various practical tips for cultivating mindfulness. One effective technique is to practice breathing exercises. Simply taking a few moments to focus on your breath can help to bring your attention to the present moment and promote a sense of calm. Spending time in nature is another way to cultivate mindfulness. Being in nature allows you to connect with your surroundings and appreciate the beauty and simplicity of the natural world.

Additionally, intentionally paying attention to one's thoughts and emotions can cultivate mindfulness. By regularly checking in with oneself and observing one's thoughts and feelings without judgment, teenagers can better understand themselves and their experiences.

Practicing mindfulness through meditation, yoga, or other activities can also be beneficial. These activities encourage a deeper connection between the mind and body, fostering a sense of unity and harmony. Regular mindfulness practices can help teenagers develop resilience and better handle the challenges of teenage life.

Spaces of Serenity: The Impact of Our Physical Environment on Our Ability To Be Mindful

Psychologists have long been intrigued by the impact of physical environments on an individual's well-being and behavior. Over the years, it has become increasingly clear that the spaces you inhabit have a deep and lasting influence on your mental health, emotions, and overall quality of life.

Consider, for example, entering a room where the atmosphere instantly puts you at ease. The carefully chosen colors, the soft and gentle lighting, and the thoughtful arrangement of furniture all work harmoniously to create a sense of tranquility. This environment has a calming effect on your mind and body, promoting relaxation and peace. It allows you to unwind, let go of stress, and recharge.

Now, imagine stepping into another space filled with activity, vibrant colors, and energetic music. The buzzing energy of the environment awakens your senses, filling you with excitement and motivation. This dynamic setting can ignite creativity, spark conversation and interaction, and inspire you to take action. It creates an atmosphere that promotes engagement and productivity.

These scenarios illustrate physical environments' profound impact on your well-being and behavior. The colors, lighting, textures, and arrangement of objects in a place can evoke specific emotions and influence our mood. Research has shown that certain colors, such as blue and green, are associated with feelings of calm and relaxation, while warm colors, like red and orange, evoke a sense of energy and excitement.

Environmental Design

The study of environmental psychology delves into how your physical surroundings impact your emotions, behaviors, and cognitive processes. It's not just coincidental that some spaces make you feel calm and at ease while others make you feel uneasy or restless. This is because deliberate design choices have the power to influence your psychological responses.

Elements like lighting, color schemes, textures, and spatial layout all significantly impact how you experience a space. For example, warm lighting and earthy tones can evoke feelings of comfort and relaxation. On the other hand, vibrant colors can stimulate energy and creativity.

Architects and designers are aware of these principles and use them strategically to create spaces that cater to specific needs. In office environments, they aim to foster productivity and collaboration by incorporating open floor plans, allowing natural light to flow in, and providing communal areas for interaction. In healthcare settings, designers focus on incorporating soothing design elements that can help reduce patient stress and promote a healing environment.

Decluttering the Mind Through Decluttering Space: How Tidiness and Organization Can Foster Clarity and Focus

The primary objective of decluttering is to combat chaos and create order in your life. By letting go of unnecessary possessions and simplifying your life, you can find happiness and lead a more straightforward existence. However, decluttering goes beyond just tidying up physical spaces. It extends to organizing other aspects of your life, such as studies, relationships, and even your digital lifestyle.

At first glance, organizing your home may not seem directly related to self-care. However, upon closer examination, you discover that self-care encompasses more than just personal grooming and pampering. In fact, organizing is a vital component of self-care. Here are several reasons why owning fewer belongings and maintaining a tidy environment can greatly improve your physical, mental, and emotional well-being.

Overcome Mental Blocks

Do you find yourself sifting through piles of clothes before finally finding the shirt you want to wear for the day? Are you constantly struggling to locate your wallet and keys on the cluttered kitchen table when you're hurrying to leave the house? Maybe there are so many boxes of trinkets in your garage that opening the door becomes daunting.

You might often tell yourself, "I'll declutter later." However, as time passes, the amount of stuff in your house, workplace, or vehicle continues to grow. If any of this sounds familiar, know that you're not alone. Many people are unaware of the significant connection between clutter and mental health.

One of the mental health benefits of decluttering is the ability to enhance your focus and overcome mental blocks. When your physical space is cluttered, it can directly impact your mental clarity and productivity. Constantly searching for items and battling clutter can leave you feeling overwhelmed and scattered. However, decluttering and organizing your surroundings free up mental energy and create a sense of order. This, in turn, allows you to focus better on your tasks and overcome the mental barriers that clutter can create.

Opportunity for Change

Getting organized is more than just a one-time task; it is a commitment to creating a life that aligns with your desires and aspirations. By decluttering and organizing your environment, you actively cultivate a space that nourishes your soul.

Rather than feeling weighed down by external factors and circumstances, organizing empowers you to take control and make intentional decisions about how you want your surroundings to be. It allows you to curate a space that reflects your values and brings you joy.

Imagine the incredible feeling of being surrounded by possessions you are genuinely proud of and that bring you happiness. With an organized environment, you can fully appreciate and enjoy the items you own. Every object serves a purpose or evokes positive emotions, eliminating any sense of clutter or dissatisfaction.

By consciously creating a space that supports your well-being and aligns with your goals, you create the potential for a fulfilling and inspiring life. Organization becomes a means of self-expression, allowing you to surround yourself with things that truly resonate with you and contribute to your overall happiness and fulfillment.

Improves Focus

When your surroundings are cluttered and disorganized, it's no wonder that you often struggle to stay focused. The presence of clutter can be visually overwhelming and mentally distracting, making it difficult to concentrate on the task at hand.

Imagine a clean and tidy workspace or living area. When everything is in its proper place, there is a sense of order and harmony. With a clutter-free environment, your visual field is simplified, allowing your mind to focus more easily.

When your surroundings are clean and organized, directing your attention and staying on track with your tasks becomes much simpler. No unnecessary distractions are pulling your focus away.

Feeling organized and in control of your surroundings positively impacts your mindset. It instills a sense of calm and clarity, creating a conducive environment for increased productivity and concentration. By eliminating clutter and creating an organized space, you set the stage for staying focused and completing your tasks more efficiently and effectively.

Nature's Role in Mindfulness: The Benefits of Integrating Natural Elements Into Our Daily Surroundings

Nature has a profound effect on your mental well-being. Scientific research has shown that exposure to natural environments offers numerous benefits, including improved creativity, problem-solving skills, and innovative thinking. When you take a break in a natural setting or incorporate elements of nature into your home, you can overcome mental blocks, stimulate your imagination, and enhance overall cognitive performance.

The beauty of nature lies in its ever-changing landscapes and intricate patterns, which arouse your curiosity and inspire you to explore new ideas and perspectives. By immersing yourself in natural environments, you tap into a wellspring of inspiration and rejuvenation.

In addition to inspiring creativity, nature also possesses remarkable healing properties for your mental health. Intentionally incorporating nature into your lives can have a transformative impact, reducing stress, boosting mood, improving cognitive function, and fostering a sense of connection and mindfulness.

Whether taking a leisurely stroll in the park, embarking on a challenging hike in the mountains, or simply spending quiet moments in your backyard, immersing yourself in the beauty of the natural world brings about profound healing. The key is to make a conscious effort to step outside, breathe in the fresh air, and allow nature to work its magic.

Mindful Rituals and Routines: Establishing Daily Habits That Promote Presence and Intentionality

Rituals and habits play a significant role in shaping your realities. They allow you to infuse mindfulness into your daily lives and embark on transformative journeys of self-exploration. In a way, your actions become a form of storytelling, as they symbolize and embody specific narratives you choose to cultivate.

Take, for example, the ritual of sitting with a cup of herbal tea at first light. This simple act can speak to the story of carving out sacred "me time" or prioritizing presence at the beginning of each day. By engaging in this ritual, you are actively participating in a narrative that inspires and educates you, shaping your beliefs and driving your actions.

You create meaning in your life through these rituals and the stories they represent. They become touchstones that ground you and provide a sense of purpose and direction. They remind you what truly matters to you and offer a framework for living in alignment with your values and aspirations.

As you consciously engage in these rituals and embrace the stories they tell, we expand your methods of being. You cultivate a deeper understanding of yourself, your desires, and your world. These rituals become transformative agents, helping you evolve, grow, and shape your realities in ways that resonate with your true self.

Mindful Techniques for Teens

Mindfulness is a practice that can greatly benefit teenagers by enhancing their awareness of their thoughts and emotions. By becoming more mindful, teenagers gain deep insights into themselves, opening up new life possibilities and choices. Central to mindfulness is the ability to observe the present moment without passing judgment. This skill allows teenagers to meet themselves with compassion and kindness, fostering a greater sense of self-acceptance and understanding.

Maintaining concentration can be challenging for teenagers in today's fast-paced world inundated with constant media stimulation. Thankfully, mindfulness provides helpful techniques and activities that promote sustained focus. Through regular practice, teenagers can develop their concentration skills, allowing them to navigate through the distractions of the modern world more effectively.

Numerous studies have demonstrated the positive impacts of mindfulness on teenagers. Firstly, it has been found to increase optimism among teens. By cultivating mindfulness, teenagers can develop a more positive outlook on life, seeing opportunities and possibilities where they might have previously seen obstacles.

Furthermore, mindfulness has been shown to improve social behaviors in teenagers. By being more aware of their thoughts and emotions, teenagers can better regulate their behavior, leading to more positive interactions with others. This greater awareness also allows them to respond to social situations with empathy and understanding, enhancing their relationships and overall social well-being.

Mindful Walking: Turning a Simple Walk Into a Grounding Exercise

When practicing mindful walking, the focus shifts from reaching a destination to being fully aware of your surroundings and your state of being. The goal is to be present in the moment, mindful of your actions, and not overly reactive or overwhelmed by external stimuli.

To make the most of your mindful walking practice, here are some tips to follow:

Start by moving slowly and consciously. Pay attention to each footstep as it rolls from heel to toe. Notice the muscles and tendons in your feet and legs, as well as the movements and sensations in the rest of your body.

Engage your senses by tuning into the environment around you. Listen to the sound of the wind blowing through the trees. Notice any scents in the air. Observe your surroundings in a soft, non-judgmental focus, paying attention to colors, textures, and movements.

Keep your attention on your breath. Breathe naturally and effortlessly without forcing deep breaths. When your mind inevitably wanders, gently guide your thoughts back to your breath.

After your mindful walking session, take a moment to stand still and take a few deep breaths. This helps transition from the walking practice and brings you back to the present moment.

If you find your mind wandering during the practice, don't be discouraged. It's common for thoughts to arise, but the key is to gently redirect your focus back to the present moment. With repeated practice, you'll find it easier to maintain a focused and present state of mind.

You may find it helpful to have a specific plan or structure for your mindful walking practice. One effective approach is to focus your awareness on different parts of your body as you walk. Here's a suggested sequence:

- Begin by bringing your attention to the soles of your feet. Rest your awareness there for a while.

- After about 20 steps (or a specific distance or time), shift your attention to your ankles and calves. Notice any sensations in this area.

- After a few minutes, shift your attention to the bend of your knees. Tune into the sensations in this part of your body.

- Next, focus on your hips and the movement of your pelvis. Notice how your body feels as you walk.

- Shift your awareness to your hands and arms. Observe whether they naturally fall at your sides or swing back and forth as you walk.

- Direct your attention to your torso, including the internal sensations of your heart and lungs. See if you notice any changes.

- Move your awareness to your neck and shoulders. Notice if there is any tension or relaxation in these areas.

- Finally, observe your head as it subtly shifts and moves with each footstep.

Continue to scan your body, noting any changes in sensation throughout your walk. This practice helps deepen your connection with your body and enhances mindfulness.

To establish mindful walking as a habit, it's helpful to create a neurological loop that reinforces the practice. This loop consists of a cue, a routine, and a reward. The cue serves as a trigger to remind you to engage in mindful walking. It could be something like having your morning cup of coffee.

The routine is the actual act of going for a mindful walk. This is where you engage in the practice of slow, intentional walking and be present in the moment. The reward is what you give yourself after completing the routine. It can be something that brings you joy or satisfaction, but it's important to provide an immediate reward to reinforce the habit.

For example, you could set up a routine where, after your morning cup of coffee, you commit to a 10-minute mindful walk in your neighborhood. As a reward, you treat yourself to a glass of your favorite freshly squeezed juice. By repeating this routine regularly, it becomes more automatic and ingrained as a habit. This is how habits are formed and maintained.

Body Scan Meditation: A Step-By-Step Method To Become Aware of Bodily Sensations and Their Emotional Connections

If you're feeling overwhelmed by the various types of meditation available, the body scan method can be a great way to start cultivating mindfulness and reaping its benefits. By engaging in a body scan meditation, you can become more attuned to the sensations in your body, which can serve as a gateway to addressing any physical or emotional issues you may be experiencing. This, in turn, can lead to improved overall wellness of both the body and mind.

Research has shown that meditation has a positive impact on physical and emotional well-being. One of the benefits is improved sleep, which can be especially helpful if you struggle with insomnia or have difficulty getting restful sleep. Meditation also offers anxiety and stress relief, providing a sense of calm and tranquility amidst the often-chaotic nature of daily life.

Another advantage of meditation is its ability to enhance self-awareness. By regularly practicing mindfulness, you become more attuned to your thoughts, emotions, and bodily sensations. This heightened self-awareness allows you to better understand yourself and your needs, which can positively influence how you navigate and respond to various situations.

Furthermore, meditation fosters self-compassion. As you develop a non-judgmental and accepting mindset through your meditation practice, you also extend that same kindness and compassion towards yourself. This can be especially valuable in cultivating a positive self-image and practicing self-care.

How to Start?

To practice a body scan meditation, follow these steps:

- Find a comfortable position: Start by getting cozy in a seated or lying position. Make sure you can stretch your limbs easily and find a position that allows you to relax.

- Focus on your breath: Close your eyes and begin to bring your attention to your breath. Notice the sensation of the breath entering and leaving your lungs as you inhale and exhale.

- Choose a starting point: Decide where you want to begin the body scan. It can be anywhere you like, such as the top of your head, your left foot, or your right hand. Focus your attention as you breathe slowly and deeply.

- Pay attention to sensations: Be aware of any sensations you may notice in that area of your body. This includes pain, discomfort, tension, or anything else that feels out of the ordinary. Take your time to observe these sensations.

- Take your time: Spend anywhere from 20 seconds to one minute observing the sensations in that part of your body. Allow yourself to fully experience and acknowledge what you are feeling.

- Acknowledge and accept emotions: If you encounter pain or discomfort, acknowledge any emotions that may arise as a result. Rather than judging or criticizing yourself for these emotions, simply observe and accept them. For example, if you feel frustration or anger, allow yourself to notice these emotions without judgment.

- Breathe through discomfort: Continue to breathe slowly and deeply, imagining the pain or tension decreasing with each breath. Visualize the breath flowing into the area of discomfort, bringing relief and relaxation.

- Release and move on: Slowly release your mental focus on that body part and redirect it to the next area of focus. Some people find it helpful to imagine releasing tension as they breathe out and moving on to the next area as they breathe in.

- Continue the scan: Continue the body scan exercise, moving along your body in a way that feels natural to you. You can choose to go from top to bottom or start from one side and move to the other. The progression is up to you.

- Note drifting thoughts: As you scan your body, you may notice your thoughts drifting or wandering. This is normal and happens to everyone. When you become aware that your mind has wandered, gently bring your attention back to where you left off with the body scan.

- Visualize and breathe: Once you have scanned all the parts of your body, let your awareness travel across your entire body. Visualize this awareness as a liquid filling a mold, moving from head to toe or from toe to head. Continue to breathe slowly and deeply as you sit with this awareness of your whole body for several seconds.

- Transition back: Slowly release your focus on the body scan and bring your attention back to your surroundings. Take a few moments to notice how you feel before slowly opening your eyes if they were closed.

Mindful Journaling: Capturing Present-Moment Thoughts and Feelings on Paper

Taking the time to capture and acknowledge your thoughts and feelings can have a transformative effect on your mental and emotional well-being. When you intentionally understand and process your inner world, you not only experience improved emotional states but also gain clarity and perspective that helps you make better sense of your experiences.

When you recognize and label your emotions, you have the power to transform big, overwhelming emotions into smaller, more manageable ones. This process diminishes the power and intensity of your emotions by interrupting the part of your brain that is responsible for generating those intense feelings. Instead, it engages your thinking brain, allowing you to step back and observe the emotion without becoming consumed by it.

Research has also shown that simply verbalizing your emotions, even if it's just saying, "I feel bad," or expressing feelings of sadness, loneliness, anxiety, or any other emotion, immediately leads to the amygdala in your brain (which detects threats) becoming less active. Consequently, it becomes less likely to trigger the stress response that often accompanies intense emotions.

By capturing your thoughts and feelings, you gain a sense of control and agency over your emotional experiences. Rather than being overwhelmed by your emotions, you can identify and label them, reducing their impact on your overall well-being. This practice allows you to navigate through life with more resilience and a greater capacity to regulate your emotions effectively. So, take the time to pause, reflect, and capture your thoughts and emotions. You'll discover the power of this simple yet impactful practice in enhancing your mental and emotional health.

Creating Mindful Routines: Incorporating Mindfulness Into Daily Activities and Habits

To find calm in the midst of chaos, it's important to tap into your basic human senses and practice mindfulness. Calming yourself is not as simple as drinking water or sitting down; it is a process that requires deliberate actions. Here are 10 mindfulness techniques that can help you find calm in your daily life:

- Play the sound game: Take a moment to listen to the sounds around you. Identify eight different sounds, whether they are from inside your body, in the room you're in, or coming from a distance. By focusing on the sounds, you can distract your mind from the chaos and bring it to the present moment.

- Ground your feet: Regardless of whether you are sitting or standing, place your feet flat on the ground. Inhale slowly for three seconds, and then exhale for three seconds. Pay attention to your breath and the sensation of your feet connecting with the floor. This technique can help you center yourself and regain a sense of stability.

- Practice introspection: Take a minute to sit still and silently evaluate your emotions. Notice each emotion that arises within you without judgment. Instead of asking yourself why you feel a certain way, focus on the question, "What do I feel?" This exercise encourages curiosity and self-awareness.

- Play the chime game: Find a quiet spot and use a bell or any object that produces a gentle sound. Ring it once and then listen attentively until you can no longer hear the sound. By directing your attention solely to the chime, you can quiet the chaos within your mind.

- Practice stillness: Engaging in stillness can slow down your racing thoughts and create a sense of calm. Choose an image or thought and concentrate on it for as long as possible. The act of focusing on something specific can help you remain still and find inner peace.

- Follow your breathing: Deep breathing is beneficial, but have you ever paid attention to the sensations as your breath travels through your body? Find a comfortable position and take a slow, deliberate breath. Follow each inhalation and exhalation, noticing where it begins, how it feels as it goes through your nose, expands your chest, and exits through your mouth. This mindful breathing can anchor you to the present moment.

- Eat slowly: Challenge yourself to savor something, such as a strawberry or a piece of chocolate, for at least 30 seconds. Pay attention to the smell, taste, and texture as you chew it. This practice of mindful eating helps you cultivate awareness and appreciate the present experience.

- Light a candle: Take a moment to light your favorite candle and observe the flame closely. Watch as it flickers and dances. While your mind may still wander, make an effort to refocus your attention on the candle. The act of observing the flame can bring a sense of tranquility and serenity.

- Play the name game: Look around your surroundings and identify three things you see, two things you hear, and one thing you feel. This exercise enhances your awareness of the present moment and helps you become more attuned to your environment.

- Walk outside: Sometimes, a breath of fresh air can be incredibly calming. If possible, go for a reflective walk outdoors or simply stick your head out of a window. Allow the fresh air to fill your lungs and take a moment to appreciate the natural surroundings. Connecting with nature can provide a soothing escape from the chaos of daily life.

By incorporating these mindfulness techniques into your daily routine, you can discover moments of calm amidst the chaos and cultivate a sense of peace and inner balance. Remember, finding calm is a continuous practice that requires your attention and commitment.

Now that you've learned some mindfulness techniques, take some time each day and perform these activities. Focus on your breathing, listen to the sounds around you, and feel your heartbeat. The point of these activities is to stay grounded in the present.

The next chapter will speak about navigating emotional triggers and how you can handle them better. Continue practicing mindfulness as you become aware of your surroundings. Look for any signs of emo-tional unrest and nip them in the bud before they escalate. While mindfulness is all about being in the present, the next chapter will speak about proactive management and understanding your emo-tional triggers. This chapter was a foundational step, and you must try to master mindfulness before diving into the next chapter.

CHAPTER 4:

Step 3 – Navigating Emotional Triggers

B y the end of this chapter, you will understand the nature and origin of emotional triggers, recognize your triggers, and possess strategies to navigate and manage these emotional surges, ensuring you respond thoughtfully rather than react impulsively. Armed with this knowledge, you'll be better equipped to maintain emotional balance in various situations, creating a foundation for healthier interpersonal relationships and self-awareness.

Have you ever found yourself suddenly overwhelmed by an emotion, seemingly out of the blue? Like a gust of wind toppling over an unsecured vase, these emotional surges can catch us off guard. The aroma of a particular perfume might transport someone back to a cherished memory, while the tone of a casual remark could sting another like a sharp slap. These are our emotional triggers, hidden and often unpredictable. But what if you could not only predict the gust of wind but also secure the vase? This chapter delves deep into the labyrinth of emotional triggers, equipping you with the tools to navigate and respond, rather than react.

Mapping Your Emotional Triggers

Emotional triggers, also known as mental health triggers or psychological triggers, are various stimuli, such as memories, objects, or people, which have the power to elicit intense negative emotions in individuals. These triggers can bring about a sudden and heightened emotional response that may seem disproportionate to the actual trigger itself.

For instance, a person who has experienced a traumatic event in the past may find that certain smells, sounds, or even specific locations evoke strong feelings of fear, anxiety, or distress. These emotional reactions can be overwhelming and often surpass what might be expected based on the trigger's inherent significance.

Understanding emotional triggers and knowing how to effectively cope with them is crucial for maintaining one's emotional well-being. By identifying and acknowledging the triggers, individuals can develop strategies to manage and minimize the impact of these emotional responses. This section will look at emotional triggers and how to deal with them.

Recognizing and Documenting What Sparks Anxiety

To effectively avoid and cope with triggers, it is essential to first identify and understand them. By recognizing what triggers your intense emotions, you can develop strategies to either avoid these triggers or manage them when they occur. Here are three tips to help you identify your triggers:

- Start a journal: Maintain a journal where you can actively record moments when you notice your anxiety or intense emotions. Note down the circumstances surrounding these instances and try to identify any patterns or common factors that may be triggering your emotional response. Some helpful apps are available that can assist you in tracking your anxiety and emotions over time, allowing you to analyze the data to identify potential triggers.

- Work with a therapist: Triggers can sometimes be challenging to identify on your own, especially if there are underlying psychological factors at play. Seeking the guidance of a mental health specialist or therapist can provide valuable insights and techniques to help you identify your triggers. They are trained professionals who may use methods like talk therapy or journaling to explore your thoughts and emotions in order to uncover hidden triggers.

- Be honest with yourself: Anxiety often leads to negative thoughts and self-doubt, which can make it challenging to identify your triggers objectively. Be patient and compassionate with yourself as you navigate this process. Acknowledge that anxious reactions can cloud your perception and understanding of triggers. Allow yourself to explore memories and experiences from your past that may be influencing your emotional responses in the present. With honesty and self-reflection, you can gain a deeper understanding of how certain events or situations impact your emotions.

Anxiety Symptoms

Anxiety can manifest itself through various symptoms that may significantly impact an individual's daily life. Some of the most common symptoms include experiencing persistent worry or fear, feeling tense or having muscle stiffness, having an accelerated heart rate, experiencing difficulty sleeping or insomnia, and struggling with concentration or focus.

If these symptoms persist and occur regularly for six months or more, it is possible that an individual may be diagnosed with generalized anxiety disorder (GAD). However, it is important to note that there are also other types of anxiety disorders, each with its own unique set of symptoms.

While there may be instances where anxiety arises seemingly out of nowhere, it is crucial to understand that there is usually an underlying cause or trigger. In some cases, the trigger may not be immediately identifiable or may lie outside of an individual's conscious awareness.

It is not uncommon for individuals with anxiety disorders to experience ongoing anxiety without fully comprehending the reasons behind it. This constant state of anxiety in the absence of a clear cause is in itself a symptom of generalized anxiety disorder. It signifies that the underlying trigger may be rooted deep within the individual's subconscious or related to various external factors that are not readily apparent.

Environmental Triggers: Understanding How Surroundings or Specific Places Can Provoke Emotions

Our mental health is influenced by numerous factors in our environment, both directly and indirectly. These environmental factors encompass various aspects of our lives, including where we live, work, go to school, and socialize.

Home

Various home-based environmental factors can have a significant impact on mental health. These factors can include the climate of your location, the amount of sunlight you are exposed to, and the occurrence of natural disasters in your area. It is important to note that climate change is also known to trigger mental health issues. The rising temperatures associated with climate change have been shown to contribute to trigger higher rates of aggression and violent suicides. Additionally, the increased frequency of natural disasters can lead to the development of depression, adjustment disorder, and post-traumatic stress disorder.

Crime levels in your area can also have a substantial impact on your mental well-being. Living in an area with a high crime rate can affect individuals, particularly females, by increasing their risk of experiencing depression and anxiety.

Another significant factor is environmental racism, which refers to racial discrimination in environmental policymaking. This form of discrimination has been identified as an important factor that negatively affects the mental health of Black, Indigenous, and People of Color (BIPOC) individuals and communities.

Long-term exposure to air pollution can also contribute to mental health issues, raising the risk of anxiety. Even short-term exposure to pollutants can increase the risk of suicide.

Furthermore, the presence of toxins inside the home, such as cleaning products and mold, can have detrimental effects on mental health. The social stress, stigma, and trauma associated with living in poverty can negatively impact the mental well-being of both children and adults. This, in turn, can lead to employment difficulties and strained relationships, creating a cycle that can be challenging to break free from for some individuals.

School

There are several school-based environmental factors that can positively impact a student's mental well-being. These factors include:

Having a sense of belonging: Feeling included and accepted within the school community is essential for a student's mental health. When a student feels like they belong, they are more likely to have positive emotional well-being and overall satisfaction with their school experience.

- Feeling connected to the school: When students feel a strong connection to their school, they are more likely to have positive attitudes towards learning and their educational environment. This can foster a sense of pride and happiness in being a part of the school community.

- Feeling safe at school: A safe and secure learning environment is crucial for student mental health. Students need to feel physically and emotionally safe in order to thrive academically and personally.

- Presence of a school-based support system: Students benefit from the availability of support systems within their school. School staff members such as teachers, school social workers, and school psychologists play a vital role in providing emotional support, guidance, and resources to students in need.

- On the other hand, certain factors can have a negative effect on a student's mental health. These include:

  - Bullying: Being subjected to bullying or harassment at school can significantly impact a student's mental well-being. It can lead to increased feelings of sadness, anxiety, and low self-esteem.

  - Lack of access to instructional materials: Limited access to proper learning resources and instructional materials

can negatively impact a student's academic performance, increase their level of educational stress, and
have detrimental effects on their mental health.

o Lack of understanding from teachers: When teachers
lack proper training or knowledge on how to address
students with mental health issues, it can create a challenging and unsupportive environment for these students, contribute to increased stress, and present difficulty in coping with their mental health concerns.

o Unclear or unfocused academic objectives: When academic goals and expectations are not clearly communicated to students, it can lead to confusion, frustration,
and a sense of overwhelm.

How To Deal With Interpersonal Triggers

Interpersonal conflict is a common occurrence in human interaction
and can arise in various degrees of severity. It arises when individuals
with different personalities, values, expectations, or problem-solving
approaches work or interact together. It is important to note that not
all conflict is negative, and learning how to navigate and resolve interpersonal conflict constructively can lead to healthier and more fulfilling
relationships.

Conflict can manifest in different ways, including verbal and nonverbal
forms. Verbal conflict involves disagreements and arguments,
whereas nonverbal conflict can be displayed through actions such as

turning away or walking away from the other person. There are six key types of interpersonal conflict.

Pseudo Conflict

Pseudo conflicts are conflicts that appear to exist but are, in reality, based on misunderstanding or miscommunication. They often occur in situations where a difference of opinion arises from a lack of clear understanding or where individuals mistakenly believe they have conflicting goals when they actually have similar objectives. Another scenario that can lead to pseudo conflicts is when one person engages in mocking or taunting behavior toward the other.

Resolving pseudo conflicts is usually relatively straightforward. It primarily requires clarification and effective communication to uncover the root of the misunderstanding or to identify the commonalities in goals. By engaging in open dialogue and actively listening to each other's perspectives, individuals can unravel the misinterpretations or misconceptions that give rise to the conflict.

It is essential to address any instances of mocking or taunting behavior in order to prevent the escalation of conflict. Teasing or badgering can often be hurtful, and most people do not enjoy being subjected to such behavior, especially in front of others. In these cases, it is crucial to have a conversation about the impact of the behavior and establish boundaries for respectful communication.

Fact Conflict

Fact conflict, also known as simple conflict, occurs when individuals have conflicting views or beliefs about factual information or the truth of a matter. In this case, the conflict arises from differing understandings of snake physiology, specifically a snake's ability to hear.

Resolving a fact conflict is relatively straightforward because it revolves around objective information. To determine the truth, you can seek out credible sources such as scientific research, expert opinions, or reputable publications. Consulting these sources can provide evidence-based information that can help resolve the conflict.

Value Conflict

Value conflicts arise when individuals have contrasting beliefs, principles, or moral values, which can be rooted in their cultural background, upbringing, personal experiences, or individual perspectives. Since personal values are deeply ingrained and shape an individual's fundamental understanding of right and wrong, finding a compromise or common ground may be challenging.

Policy Conflict

Policy conflict occurs when individuals are unable to reach a consensus regarding the approach or action plan to resolve a particular problem or situation. This conflict arises due to a variety of factors such as personality traits, upbringing, educational background, and other personal influences, all of which shape an individual's perspective on policy-making or problem-solving. It is important to note that encountering policy conflicts is a common occurrence, given the diverse range of perspectives and experiences that people bring to the table.

Ego Conflict

Have you ever found yourself in a situation where you and the other person involved in an argument stubbornly refuse to back down or accept defeat? This type of scenario often involves ego conflict, which tends to complicate and intensify any disagreement. Ego conflict typically arises alongside other forms of conflict, and it frequently occurs when the conflict becomes personal.

In these situations, it is common for individuals, including yourself or others involved, to attach their intelligence or self-worth to the outcome of the conflict. This can lead to heated exchanges where judgmental or derogatory remarks are used as a means to gain the upper hand. Unfortunately, when the focus shifts to the ego conflict, attempts to resolve the underlying issue at hand tend to be derailed.

Meta Conflict

Meta conflict occurs when conflicts arise regarding how conflicts themselves are handled or communicated. It is a situation where individuals find themselves engaging in conflict about the very nature of their conflicts. This type of conflict often arises when communication issues come to the forefront.

For instance, a common example of meta conflict is when one person accuses the other of never truly listening despite nodding in agreement during discussions. The accused might counter that the accusation is irrelevant and not reflective of the actual topic being discussed. Another instance could involve one individual expressing frustration with the other's emotional state during a conflict, stating that they can't handle the person when they are in that heightened state.

Resolving conflicts effectively requires clear and productive communication. However, meta conflict tends to hinder this process, as it brings up issues related to communication in unhelpful ways.

Internal Triggers vs. External Triggers

Triggers can vary greatly from person to person and can be categorized as either internal or external. Internal triggers originate within an individual and can manifest as memories, physical sensations, or emotions.

Internal Triggers

An internal trigger originates from within. For example, during exercise, if your heart starts pounding, this physical sensation might remind you of a time when you were nervous about the results for an exam or maybe escaping abusive friends at school (bullying). Other common internal triggers include feelings of anger, anxiety, being overwhelmed, vulnerable, abandoned, or out of control, experiencing loneliness, muscle tension, memories associated with a traumatic event, pain, or sadness.

External Triggers

On the other hand, external triggers stem from the person's environment and can be attributed to specific people, places, or situations. What might seem like a normal, everyday situation or a minor inconvenience to some can be triggering for someone living with a mental illness.

For instance, an individual who has experienced trauma may be triggered by encountering:

- Media content such as movies, television shows, or news articles that remind them of their traumatic experience.

- Interactions with individuals connected to the traumatic event, such as arguing with a friend, spouse, or partner.

- Specific times of the day that coincide with the incident or bring back painful memories.

- Certain sounds that evoke recollections of the traumatic event.

- Changes in relationships or the ending of a relationship.

- Significant dates, such as holidays or anniversaries, serve as reminders of past traumas.

- Visiting a particular location that triggers memories associated with the traumatic event.

- Smells, like the smell of smoke, which are associated with the traumatic experience.

Managing Digital or Media Triggers

We are currently living in the information age, where access to a vast array of knowledge and resources is readily available to us through the internet and technology. Scientific discoveries, economic data, and expert opinions on any topic we are curious about can be found with just a few clicks. It is a time when answers to almost any question we have are within reach.

However, along with the benefits of being constantly connected to this wealth of information, there are also downsides. Our smartphones are always within arm's reach, constantly buzzing with notifications from emails, text messages, and social media updates. Many of us rely on computers for our day-to-day work responsibilities. And it is not un-common for homes to have multiple televisions, offering a continuous stream of entertainment and news.

For survivors of child sexual abuse, this reliance on technology and constant exposure to media poses a significant challenge. The risk of encountering triggering content or reminders of their abuse is high. It could be as simple as scrolling through Instagram and coming across a photo that reminds them of someone involved in their abuse. Even watching a favorite TV show can be disrupted by a sudden news re-port about another celebrity being accused of sexual misconduct.

As society becomes even more saturated with technology and discus-sions surrounding sexual violence continue to make headlines, it be-comes crucial for survivors to learn how to recognize and manage these triggers. Ignoring them can have a detrimental impact on their healing journey and may affect their ability to function in certain environments. It is essential to develop strategies to navigate these challenges and seek support when needed to ensure emotional well-being and continued progress in healing.

Strategies for Diffusing Triggers

Throughout history, our ancestors have learned to adapt and survive by creating tools to meet their needs. Nowadays, we have a wide range of tools at our disposal, including psychological and spiritual methods, to help us respond rather than react to the triggers we encounter in our lives.

The first tool is to name our triggers. This involves recognizing the specific people, words, places, or behaviors that frequently activate emotional responses within us. By keeping a written list of these triggers, we become more aware and prepared to consciously respond to them instead of reacting impulsively.

The second tool is to seek the source of our trigger reactions. By identifying the specific events or traumas that are at the root of our triggers, we can begin to free ourselves from their grasp. Understanding the connection between our past experiences and our present triggers allows us to better navigate and lessen their impact on us.

Projection is a key concept to be aware of when it comes to triggers. Our reactions are often projections of past experiences onto current situations. For example, if we experienced anger and violence from a parent in the past, we may be triggered by anger in others today, even if there is no direct correlation between the two. Recognizing this tendency to project can help us take ownership of our reactions and empower ourselves to heal from the original wounds.

When triggered, our bodies release stress hormones such as cortisol and adrenaline, causing us to feel fragile, disoriented, and unable to self-regulate. It is important to notice these signs of hyperarousal and employ relaxation techniques to calm ourselves down. Taking deep breaths, going for a walk, or splashing cold water on our faces can help ground us in the present moment and reduce the intensity of our reactions.

Instead of engaging in arguments with our inner critic, we can use its voice as a signal for self-care. By acknowledging the critical voice and responding with affirmations or self-soothing practices, we can break free from its negative influence and cultivate self-trust.

Practicing emotional awareness and expression is crucial in handling triggers. Emotions are like muscles that need to be used appropriately in order to develop healthily. If we have suppressed certain emotions, they may resurface in exaggerated or awkward ways when triggered. By allowing ourselves to fully know and express our emotions, we become better equipped to respond appropriately to strong feelings.

Losing objectivity is a common experience when triggered. Stepping away from the situation for a brief moment can help regain perspective and calm the ego. This distance allows us to communicate nonjudgmentally about the effects certain actions or experiences have on us.

If someone is shaming or insulting us, an echo response can be employed. This involves calmly repeating the triggering words back to the person who said them. This pause disrupts the negative impact of the words and redirects the energy back to its source, preventing us from feeling victimized.

Family members often know our triggers and have a knack for pushing our buttons. Being aware of this dynamic and staying present in such situations can help us maintain boundaries while still approaching them with love. When tensions escalate, it may be necessary to remove ourselves temporarily from the environment to protect our well-being.

Finding humor in triggering situations can be a powerful tool to diffuse stress. It allows us to shift our perspective and find lightness in challenging circumstances. Remembering that everyone experiences triggers can help alleviate the feeling of isolation. Knowing that even those we trust and admire are impacted by triggers can lessen their power over us and remind us that we are not alone in our struggles.

Seeking professional help is essential if we find that a particular trigger is causing unmanageable stress. Therapies such as somatic therapy and EMDR can assist in integrating past traumas into our present awareness, facilitating healing and growth.

Ultimately, practicing acceptance is key in handling triggers. Acknowledging that triggering events will happen and that we cannot change others' actions or words allows us to be kinder to ourselves. While abuse should never be accepted, accepting the reality of triggers occurring in life helps us regain control over our responses and find peace within ourselves.

The Role of Memory in Triggers

Memory is a complex cognitive process that involves three main operations: Encoding, storing, and retrieving information. Encoding refers to the process of learning and acquiring information. Once information is encoded, it can either be stored in short-term memory or transferred to long-term memory in the brain. Short-term memories are temporary and can be quickly forgotten, while long-term memory has unlimited storage capacity.

The process of retrieval involves accessing and recalling stored memories. Even if we do not consciously try to recall something, stimuli from our environment, such as sights or sounds, can trigger the retrieval of long-term memories.

Interestingly, our brains are more likely to remember information that is associated with intense emotions compared to routine facts that tend to be forgotten. Numerous studies have shown that people are better at recalling information that is linked to strong positive or negative emotions, as compared to neutral information. The emotional relevance of a memory plays a significant role in its retention or forgetting.

When it comes to forgetting a distressing memory, it is often not the memory itself that is forgotten, but rather, the associated negative emotions are gradually separated from the memory. Various techniques and therapies aim to help individuals detach the negative emotions from traumatic memories, allowing them to remember the event without the overwhelming emotions that were initially associated with it.

Empowering Through Education

When trying to address a specific behavior, it is important to consider what triggers that behavior. For example, by understanding the triggers, parents can better understand why their child may be acting out and can also take steps to prevent those behaviors from happening in the first place. Additionally, it is helpful to identify the triggers that lead to positive behaviors, such as obeying commands. Here are some potential triggers that parents should avoid:

- Assuming expectations are understood: It is possible that children may not fully understand what is expected of them, even if parents assume they do. Expectations can vary from situation to situation, and when children are unsure of what they are supposed to do, they are more likely to misbehave. It is important to clearly communicate expectations and ensure that children understand them.

- Calling out instructions from a distance: When giving important instructions, it is best to be face-to-face with the child. Instructions that are yelled from a distance are less likely to be remembered and understood. By taking the time to establish direct communication, parents can increase the chances of their instructions being followed.

- Transitioning without warning: This can be difficult for children, especially when they are in the middle of something they're enjoying. It is helpful to give children a warning before transitioning and allow them time to find a good stopping place. By doing so, transitions can be less stressful for children, and they are more likely to cooperate.

- Asking rapid-fire questions or giving a series of instructions: Presenting a barrage of questions or instructions at once reduces the likelihood that children will be able to process and respond to each one. It becomes difficult for them to remember the tasks and carry out the instructions effectively. To maximize comprehension and compliance, it is important to deliver instructions and questions one at a time, allowing the child to fully process each one before moving on to the next.

I hope you have a clear understanding of triggers. You should be able to anticipate triggers and react better. Ask yourself these questions: Who triggers a negative reaction within you? How do you cope with a situation you don't want to be in? Once you've identified your triggers, come up with reactions that can help you manage your emotional response. It's important to plan so you respond better.

When exploring emotions, it can be helpful to use common songs as a starting point. For example, songs like "If You're Happy and You Know It" convey a sense of happiness, while "Twinkle Twinkle Little Star" conveys a feeling of curiosity. These songs serve as fun and engaging ways to introduce and discuss emotions with children.

In addition to these common songs, there are many other songs and activities that you can enjoy to further explore emotions. Here are a few suggestions:

"The Wheels on the Bus": This song can be used to discuss different emotions that passengers on the bus might experience. For example, singing about the "happy driver" or the "crying baby" allows children to identify and understand different emotions.

Puppet Shows: Use puppets to act out various emotional scenarios and encourage children to identify and discuss the emotions being portrayed. This interactive activity allows children to express themselves and understand different emotional states.

Now that you've learned about emotional triggers, you're capable of controlling your reaction better. This was one of the first layers. The next chapter will discuss how to combat anxiety and help you react better. The chapter will provide techniques you can always rely on.

CHAPTER 5:

Step 4 - Hassle-Free Techniques to Combat Anxiety

I n this chapter, you will discover practical and effective techniques to overcome anxiety and restore emotional balance. By the end of this chapter, you will be equipped with a toolkit of strategies to manage and alleviate anxiety in various situations.

Envision a serene shoreline where the ebb and flow of waves mirror the rise and fall of worries and fears. Standing at the water's edge, you realize that just as a skilled sailor harnesses the wind, you too can wield techniques that grant you mastery over anxiety's tumultuous currents. In this chapter, embark on a voyage of discovery as you chart a course toward calmer waters using hassle-free techniques that empower you to navigate anxiety's tide.

Breathing Through the Stress

If you're feeling stressed or anxious and need ways to relax, there are various types of breathing techniques that can help you feel calmer. These exercises are simple and can be done in a quiet space where you can focus on your breath.

It's important to note that these exercises don't have to take up a lot of time. Just a few minutes dedicated to paying attention to your breathing can make a difference. Here are some suggestions to get started:

- Start with five minutes a day and gradually increase the duration as you become more comfortable with the exercises.

- If five minutes seems too long initially, start with just two minutes and gradually work your way up.

- Practice multiple times a day. You can set specific times for breathing exercises or do them whenever you feel the need for relaxation.

Why Does Deep Breathing Work?

Deep breathing is a powerful tool for calming the body in times of stress or anxiety. When someone takes shallow, short breaths from their chest, it can induce a state of anxiety or panic, known as hyperventilation. On the other hand, purposeful deep breathing can have the opposite effect and physically calm the body down.

The reason deep breathing works is due to the functioning of the autonomic system. This system is responsible for actions like digestion and heart rate. This system is divided into two parts: The sympathetic system and the parasympathetic system. The sympathetic system controls the fight-or-flight response. On the other hand, the parasympathetic system controls the rest-and-relax response.

Both parts of the nervous system are always active, but deep breathing can help quiet the sympathetic nervous system. By engaging in deep, intentional breaths, you can activate the parasympathetic nervous system and reduce feelings of stress or anxiety. This makes deep breathing a helpful practice not only for managing day-to-day anxiety but also for addressing more pervasive issues like generalized anxiety disorder.

Practicing Deep Breathing

Deep breathing involves intentionally taking slower but longer breaths from your stomach as opposed to the short, rapid breaths that occur naturally when you're stressed or anxious.

To practice deep breathing, find a comfortable position, close your eyes, and imagine an extremely stressful situation to activate your sympathetic nervous system. Pay attention to how your body responds: You may feel tightness in your chest, shallow breathing, and a faster heartbeat.

Next, shift your focus to your breath. Start breathing from your stomach, allowing your stomach to expand with each inhale. Take longer breaths. Count to at least three for both the inhalation and exhalation. Initially, this might feel uncomfortable, but continue practicing. Over time, you'll begin to notice your body becoming more relaxed and at ease.

Deep breathing is a simple technique, but it requires practice. While it may not instantly relieve all anxiety, it can quickly calm your nervous system. The more you practice deep breathing, the better you'll become at it, and you'll be able to utilize it effectively during times of stress to help bring a sense of calm and relaxation.

Deep Breathing for Anxiety

Deep breathing techniques can vary, so it's important to find one that feels natural and comfortable for you.

One approach is to inhale till you count to four, then exhale till you count to six. This ratio of inhaling for a shorter duration and exhaling for a longer duration can promote a sense of relaxation and calmness.

Another technique to try is square breathing. Inhale, hold your breath for four seconds, exhale till you count to four, and then hold again for a count of four. This method involves equal durations for each phase of the breath and can help bring a sense of balance and centeredness.

Ultimately, the specific pattern or ratio you choose is less important than maintaining slow and deep breaths. Finding a rhythm that works best for you is key, so feel free to experiment and discover what feels most natural and effective in promoting relaxation and reducing stress.

Be Mindful

Mindfulness is an integral aspect of deep breathing practice that can enhance its effectiveness. It involves consciously bringing awareness to your emotions and the physical sensations occurring in your body without attaching any judgment or labeling them as "good" or "bad."

When practicing deep breathing mindfully, direct your attention solely to your breath. Allow any thoughts that arise to naturally fade away without giving them further attention. It's important not to criticize or judge yourself for having thoughts but also refrain from actively following or engaging with them. Instead, strive to release and let go of any thoughts that arise, allowing your focus to remain on the breath and the present moment.

By cultivating a non-judgmental and non-reactive attitude toward your thoughts, you can develop a greater sense of presence and mindfulness during your deep breathing practice. This allows you to fully immerse yourself in the experience of your breath and further enhance the calming and stress-reducing benefits of deep breathing.

Grounding Oneself in the Present

Grounding oneself in the present is an important practice for maintaining emotional well-being. There are several activities that can help achieve this, including walking in nature, running, and practicing yoga.

Taking a leisurely walk in nature can have a profound impact on your emotional health. Studies have shown that spending time outdoors can lower stress levels, elevate mood, and improve overall mental well-being. The combination of gentle exercise, fresh air, and the calming effects of nature creates a peaceful atmosphere that promotes relaxation and tranquility.

Running is another fantastic activity for promoting emotional health. During cardiovascular exercise, your body releases endorphins, often referred to as "feel-good" hormones. These endorphins can improve your mood, reduce tension and anxiety, and create an overall sense of happiness. Running also provides an opportunity for reflection, allowing you to process your feelings and unwind.

Yoga is a practice that combines physical postures, breath control, and mindfulness to enhance emotional well-being. Through gentle stretching, controlled breathing, and focused attention, yoga cultivates self-awareness, mental clarity, and stress reduction. Regular practice of yoga can induce a state of relaxation, regulate emotions, and foster a sense of inner peace and contentment.

Harnessing Positive Distractions

Art therapy is a powerful form of mental health treatment that utilizes various art media to help patients therapeutically process and understand their emotions. Traditionally, art therapy involves working with a licensed therapist to address a wide range of issues, from rehabilitation to processing past trauma. However, there are also art therapy exercises that you can do on your own to help reduce stress and promote emotional well-being.

One popular form of art therapy is ceramics and clay work. Working with clay can be an intimate and focused experience that helps people practice mindfulness and create delicate designs. This process allows the mind to focus on the activity of molding and shaping rather than stressors or other negative emotions.

Another effective art therapy exercise is sculpting. Sculpting can be a valuable tool for therapists to observe how patients work with their sculptures and to understand them better. It is also a great activity to help promote focus and concentration, which can reduce stress and anxiety.

Lastly, doodling and scribbling are also effective methods of exercising emotions and anxiety. Many people who struggle with nervousness find themselves doodling or scribbling absentmindedly in other public settings. These activities can help promote a sense of calmness and control during stressful situations.

Building a Toolkit for Anxiety

In order to perform effective visualization, creating an environment that prevents distractions is key. Find a comfortable space in which you can fully focus on your mental imagery and consider factors like lighting, temperature, and noise levels. Personalizing this space with inspirational quotes or imagery relevant to your sport or activity can also be beneficial, as it creates a sanctuary where you can fully immerse yourself without disruptions.

Another prerequisite to effective visualization is relaxation. Utilizing techniques such as progressive muscle relaxation or deep breathing exercises can be highly effective in achieving a relaxed state. With progressive muscle relaxation, you systematically tense and release each muscle group to promote relaxation. Deep breathing exercises help anchor the mind, easing tension and stress and bringing the mind to a neutral, focused state.

When visualizing, it is important to make the visualization as vivid as possible. This means that your visualization should involve all of your senses, not just your visual sense. For example, if you are visualizing as a basketball player, your mental imagery should include the squeak of your shoes on the hardwood, the weight of the ball in your hands, the smell of the court, and the roar of the crowd as you make the winning shot. The more realistic your mental imagery, the more your brain responds as though the action is actually happening, which makes the visualization more effective.

After learning all about controlling anxiety, practice it with a breathing session. Breathing plays an important role in calming your emotional reaction. It also helps calm the nervous system. As teens, you should practice deep breathing. It's an effective yet simple technique where you inhale through the nose, pause for a bit, and exhale slowly.

You will be able to control your emotions and reactions better with the help of this simple technique. This was another successful step towards your deep inner journey. The sixth chapter will speak about the inner voice and how these self-conversations can transform you from within.

CHAPTER 6:

Step 5 - Conversations with Self

B y the end of this chapter, you will comprehend the profound impact of internal dialogue on emotional well-being, self-worth, and overall mental health. You'll gain techniques to re-shape this dialogue, transforming it from a potential adversary to your strongest ally.

Every day, within the silent chambers of our minds, a continuous conversation unfolds, unseen and unheard by others. This inner dialogue, which can be both our harshest critic and most ardent supporter, profoundly influences our emotional landscape. As we approach the final yet pivotal step of our transformative journey, it becomes imperative to master this dialogue. How often have we allowed this internal voice to dictate our self-worth, decisions, and mood? In this chapter, we'll delve into strategies to effectively harness this conversation, transforming it into a powerful ally for emotional resilience and self-discovery.

Challenging the Inner Critic

Self-talk refers to the way you talk to yourself internally, often without even realizing it. It is the combination of conscious thoughts, beliefs, and biases that create an ongoing internal monologue throughout the day.

The importance of self-talk lies in its significant impact on how you feel and what you do. It can be either supportive and beneficial, motivating you, or negative, undermining your confidence.

Your self-talk can greatly influence your mental health and your relationships with others. If you constantly think negatively about yourself, you will likely feel bad most of the time. This negativity can drag you down and make it difficult to bounce back from low points. Individuals experiencing depression or anxiety often find themselves caught in a constant stream of negative self-talk, which can feel overwhelming and challenging to escape.

Moreover, negative self-talk can make it harder to cope with chronic pain, affect your sexual confidence and body image, and contribute to stress and perfectionism. Negative self-talk tends to become repetitive and overpowering, often appearing to be true. To break free from this cycle, consider these tips:

Become aware of what you are saying to yourself. Simply pausing and recognizing negative thoughts for what they are is the first step toward addressing the issue. Ask yourself if you would talk to someone else in the same way.

Challenge your thoughts. Question their validity and ask yourself if they are really true. Often, negative thoughts are not based on reality. Consider alternative explanations or different perspectives. Remind yourself that many of the things you worry about never actually happen. Negative self-talk tends to exaggerate situations.

Put your thoughts into perspective. Ask yourself, "So what?" Try to view things from a different angle and possibly from another person's perspective. You can also try writing your thoughts down or saying them out loud. Finally, ask yourself if the situation will truly matter in a few years.

Stop the negative thoughts. You can employ a visualization technique called "thought stopping" by imagining the thought being halted or squashed. Alternatively, you can create a ritual to interrupt the negative thought pattern.

Replace the negative thought with a positive or neutral thought. Ask yourself, "What is a more helpful thought?" Focus on finding alternative ways to interpret the situation that are more supportive and constructive.

Affirmations for Self-Understanding

Affirmations are powerful statements that you repeat to yourself either verbally or mentally. Despite appearing as simple words, affirmations have a profound impact on your subconscious mind.

When you consistently recite affirmations, you are effectively introducing a new thought into your mind. With enough repetition, this new thought takes root and grows, eventually becoming your dominant belief about yourself. As your self-beliefs change, so does your reality.

Negative self-talk, such as, "I'm not good enough" or "I'll never be successful," can be detrimental to your progress and hinder your ability to achieve your goals. However, by replacing these negative thoughts with positive affirmations like, "I am worthy," or "I am capable," you create space to embrace new possibilities and open yourself up to success.

The Role of Self-Reflection

Engaging in self-reflection allows us to develop an inner witness within ourselves. This inner witness enables us to observe ourselves, including our thoughts and what lies beneath them, from a slight distance. It is akin to looking at our reflection in a mirror, although the significance of self-reflection goes far beyond our physical appearance.

Through self-reflection, we direct our attention to ourselves with interest, curiosity, and inquiry, particularly when we're exploring our behaviors, thoughts, and emotions. Initially, we become aware of what we are feeling in our bodies, experiencing in our emotions, and thinking in our minds. This awareness forms the core content of our experience. However, the true value of self-reflection lies in our ability to delve deeper by asking ourselves probing questions:

- How did this thought come about?
- What truly underlies my declaration of sadness?
- Is there something even deeper than this feeling of anxiety?

- What do these sensations in my body express about my perception of my situation?

Self-reflection serves as a vital skill for personal growth. Without it, we remain unaware and often react to others and even ourselves without conscious intention. If you have ever experienced an emotional reaction or regretted something you said in the heat of the moment, you can recognize how self-reflection can support you in choosing more healthy responses and changing behaviors and even thoughts that are not serving you well. Through self-reflection, we become more conscious, responsive, and empowered in our own lives.

Establishing a Dialogue with the Future Self

Creating a mental image of your future self and desired reality is a crucial step in achieving your goals.

Visualization is a practice that you may already engage in regularly, leading you to question the need for a lesson on it. Alternatively, it might seem too intangible to warrant significant time and attention.

However, we encourage you to dedicate time to mastering the art of visualization. This skill is the beginning of a transformative journey toward creating the world you truly desire. The primary beneficiary of this process is you. By gaining clarity on your desires and understanding the "what" and "why" behind them, you can effectively determine the "how" of achieving them.

Visualization is more than just daydreaming. It involves actively creating detailed mental images of your desired future, allowing you to fully immerse yourself in that reality. Visualization enhances your ability to connect with your goals, increasing your motivation, focus, and belief in your ability to achieve them.

By consistently practicing visualization techniques, you strengthen the connection between your mind and your desired reality. This mental rehearsal prepares you for the challenges and opportunities that lie ahead, helping you make informed decisions and take effective actions to bring your aspirations to life.

Remember, visualization is a powerful tool that empowers you to shape your destiny. Embrace this practice as a valuable step towards creating the world you want to live in.

To integrate affirmations and positive self-talk into your daily routine, consider the following detailed tips:

- Wake up and recite your affirmations out loud: Start your day by standing in front of a mirror or finding a quiet space where you can say your affirmations aloud with intention and conviction.

- Write your affirmations in a journal or notebook: Take the time to physically write down your affirmations. This process enhances the connection between your mind and the words on the page. Make it a habit to read them out loud daily, reinforcing their positive impact.

- Create a vision board or collage: Use images, words, and colors to visually represent your affirmations. Place the vision board or collage in a prominent location, such as your bedroom or workspace, where you can see it daily. Allow the visuals to instill a sense of motivation and inspiration.

- Use screensavers or backgrounds: Customize the screensavers or backgrounds on your electronic devices with your affirmations. This way, you'll be reminded of your positive statements every time you unlock your phone or open your computer.

- Listen to affirmation audio recordings: Find pre-recorded affirmation audios that resonate with you or create your personalized recordings. Listen to these affirmations during your commute, while exercising, or whenever you need a boost of positivity throughout the day.

- Carry affirmations with you: Write your affirmations on a small card or slip of paper and keep it in your wallet, pocket, or purse. Whenever you have a free moment, take it out and read your affirmations as a reminder of your intentions and self-belief.

- Recite affirmations in front of a mirror: Stand in front of a mirror and articulate your affirmations confidently. The act of seeing yourself say the words adds a powerful dimension to the practice and reinforces self-acceptance and positivity.

- Practice affirmations with a friend or family member: Share your affirmations with someone you trust and invite them to join you in reciting their affirmations. This practice can strengthen your bond, provide support, and create a positive environment for personal growth.

Internal dialogue is all about the power of perceptions and emotions. While mastering the conversation with yourself is just the beginning, you need to understand the underlying layer to this and how it's rooted in your values and beliefs. The next chapter will take it further and help you understand yourself better.

CHAPTER 7:

Cultivating Deep Self-Understanding

By the end of this chapter, you will recognize the foundational pillars that constitute your true self, which include personal beliefs, experiences, and intrinsic values. You'll also acquire strategies to dissect these foundations, leading to profound self-awareness and empowering you to make choices more aligned with your authentic selves.

Imagine walking through a dense forest where every tree represents a belief, value, or experience that defines you. Some trees stand tall, symbolizing the positive affirmations and proud moments of your life, while others might appear withered, echoing past regrets or detrimental beliefs. This forest forms the essence of who you are, and understanding each tree helps you navigate life with a deeper sense of purpose and clarity. Chapter 7 is about mapping this forest, ensuring you not only recognize every tree but also understand its roots and significance in your life's larger landscape. Dive in and discover the transformative power of deep self-understanding.

Embracing Self-Compassion

Self-love, the acceptance and appreciation of oneself, is a crucial element of mental and emotional well-being. Numerous studies have highlighted its significance in improving mental health, increasing resilience, and fostering positive relationships.

One of the notable benefits of self-love is its positive impact on mental health. Research has found that individuals who practice self-love tend to experience lower levels of depression and anxiety. By accepting and appreciating themselves, individuals are able to reduce negative self-talk and alleviate negative emotions. Additionally, self-love contributes to increased self-esteem, which plays a pivotal role in maintaining good mental health.

Furthermore, self-love enhances resilience, which refers to the ability to bounce back from adversity. Studies have demonstrated that individuals who cultivate self-love are better equipped to cope with stress and navigate challenging circumstances. Furthermore, these individuals are more likely to seek support and engage in healthier coping strategies. Self-love empowers individuals to view themselves as capable and deserving of assistance.

Self-love also plays a crucial role in fostering healthy relationships. Research has indicated that individuals who practice self-love tend to have more fulfilling relationships with their partners, friends, and family members. This is because self-love enables individuals to communicate effectively and establish healthy boundaries. Moreover, self-love allows individuals to maintain realistic expectations within relationships, leading to increased satisfaction and decreased conflict.

So, how do you cultivate self-love? Research suggests several effective strategies. One such strategy is self-compassion, which involves treating oneself with kindness and understanding when faced with personal failure or inadequacy. Self-compassion entails recognizing that suffering and setbacks are part of the human experience and extending the same empathy to oneself that one would offer to a close friend.

Another way to cultivate self-love is through positive self-talk. By consciously replacing negative self-talk with supportive and uplifting thoughts, individuals can bolster their self-esteem and improve their mental well-being. Moreover, practicing gratitude is a powerful technique for nurturing self-love. Focusing on the things one is grateful for in life helps shift the attention from negative thoughts to more positive ones.

Self-love is a vital aspect of mental and emotional well-being. By embracing self-acceptance and appreciation, individuals can experience improved mental health, increased resilience, and more fulfilling relationships. Integrating practices such as self-compassion, positive self-talk, and gratitude into daily life can facilitate the cultivation of self-love and contribute to overall well-being.

Reflecting on Growth and Resilience

Taking the time to celebrate our growth allows us to reflect on how much progress we have made. It can be a powerful experience to step back and recognize all the changes we have made in our lives. This reflection gives us a clear perspective on where we have been and where we are heading.

Noticing and appreciating the things that are going well in our lives can remind us of the many reasons to celebrate. Often, we are so focused on our goals and continuously working towards them that we forget to acknowledge the little joys along the way. By taking a moment to celebrate our growth, we can fully embrace and enjoy the journey.

It is important to recognize that progress is ongoing. As we achieve one goal, we often find ourselves setting new ones. If we wait until we have achieved all our goals before celebrating, we may never give ourselves the chance. It is essential to permit ourselves to celebrate the growth we have already achieved, even as we continue to strive for more. So, amidst the hustle of pursuing our next goal, it is vital to take a step back and acknowledge the progress we have made.

Developing Intuition and Inner Wisdom

Have you ever experienced a feeling deep in your gut, or a nagging sensation that something is not quite right? Perhaps you have felt a sudden surge of clarity and calmness after making a decision. These are examples of a gut instinct; an innate ability we all possess. Your body communicates with you through gut feelings, providing both positive and negative responses, attempting to convey something important.

Gut instincts can manifest in various ways, and each person may experience them differently. Some common signs of a gut feeling include the sensation of "butterflies" or nausea in the stomach, clammy or sweaty palms, tension or tightness in muscles, a sinking feeling or a sense of calm in the chest, a sudden surge of clarity, vivid dreams, or an increased heart rate.

There is a misconception that gut feelings are solely based on emotion and, therefore, cannot be trusted. It is understandable why people may hold this belief. Gut instincts seem to emerge out of nowhere and lack tangible evidence to support them. They come in different forms, often leaving individuals feeling unsettled or unexplainably calm. How can we trust such volatile physical responses?

However, gut responses are not as whimsical as they may first appear. They are, in fact, highly curated and developed from exposure to various stimuli and life events. They are the result of a complex filing system within your brain, assisted by your gut. This filing system consists of an unconscious library of memories and fragments that you may have no recollection of attaining.

Your brain then utilizes these stored memories of past experiences to predict what may happen next when encountering a series of events or stimuli that resemble those memories. The effects of this predicted event are then felt throughout your body, often triggering a fight or flight response. It becomes a question of whether to take a risk or not based on your body's interpretation of the predicted outcome.

Reconnecting with Core Values

Do you wish to live a more meaningful and fulfilling life that connects to your deeper self? The answer may be harder than you think, as it dwells within you through discovering your values. Your values play a fundamental role in defining what a meaningful life looks like to you.

Your values serve as a justification for the person you are at your deepest, most personal level. They are the principles that guide your decisions, behaviors, and actions. Furthermore, your values could even aid in healing from various conditions. Researchers suggest that several evidence-based treatments employ values as the basis for treating depression.

In a world that moves at a fast pace, it's entirely understandable if you feel disconnected from your values or like you're at the mercy of others' agendas and desires for you. However, identifying your core values makes it easier to move forward confidently without being held back by fear, anxiety, or negative thoughts. Knowledge of your values allows you to continue pursuing important, inspiring projects, activities, or adventures.

The values you hold can motivate you to give a poignant speech, write a book that helps someone through a painful time, or travel to a fascinating bucket-list location. Your core values serve as the fuel that keeps you moving in the direction you set out to go, even when self-doubt or jitters appear.

Similarly, your core values serve as resistance bands against potentially overwhelming emotions such as anger, frustration, or jealousy. They guide you in taking action on what you hold dear, assisting you in resolving conflicts or mending relationships.

Before I end the chapter, let's envision the forest again. How do you want it to look in the future? What beliefs do you want to grow on it? Which trees will you reshape or prune? Doing so will give you a roadmap for growth. Your actions will align with your true self.

At this stage of the book, you will have become adept at recognizing and labeling emotions. You will also have a clear idea of your true self. This is part of the journey, and you will keep evolving with time. The next chapter will be the final one in this guide. It will serve as a launchpad for continued growth.

CHAPTER 8:

The Journey Continues

By the end of this chapter, you will recognize that self-awareness and emotional growth are continuous endeavors. You'll be equipped with strategies for lifelong learning and introspection, understanding that every chapter of life offers opportunities to reapply and refine the principles you've discovered.

Like ripples in a pond after a stone has been cast, the journey of self-understanding and emotional mastery doesn't stop at the point of impact; it continues, ever-expanding, touching every corner of our existence. We've navigated the complexities of emotions and conversed deeply with our inner selves. Now, as we stand on the brink of endless possibilities, it's crucial to remember that this is not the end but merely the beginning of a lifelong voyage. Embrace it with the tools and wisdom acquired, for the real journey, one filled with revelations and growth has just commenced.

A Lifelong Commitment to Self-Understanding

Emotional maturity involves having the ability to effectively manage and understand your emotions. It means not viewing emotions as a weakness but instead appreciating their value and being willing to acknowledge and express them. Emotionally mature individuals recognize the importance of learning from past experiences and are willing to explore and understand their emotions, even if it is difficult to let go of them. This level of emotional intelligence is a strong indicator of emotional maturity.

It is essential to understand that emotional maturity is not something that can be achieved overnight or maintained without effort. It is an ongoing process that requires sustained dedication and perseverance throughout all stages of life.

Just like physical and mental maturity, emotional maturity is a continuous journey. Our bodies go through different stages of physical maturity from infancy to adulthood, and our cognitive skills develop over time. Similarly, our emotional maturity evolves as we grow and gain better control over our emotions. As we progress from childhood to adolescence and adulthood, we learn to express ourselves with words and reflect on our actions, moving away from impulsive, emotional reactions.

Recognizing signs of emotional immaturity can help us identify specific areas for growth and improvement. Here are four signs of emotional immaturity to consider:

- **Incapable of expressing emotions:** If you consistently find it challenging to connect with and express your own emotions, avoiding vulnerability at all costs, it may indicate emotional immaturity. Difficulty admitting negative experiences and expressing feelings suggests a need for emotional growth.

- **Blaming others:** When faced with challenging situations, emotionally immature individuals tend to automatically place blame on others, absolving themselves of responsibility. Avoiding accountability, even when knowing it is their fault, is a telling sign of immaturity.

- **Reluctance to ask for help:** Immaturity can also be seen in the reluctance to seek assistance when it is needed the most. Fear of appearing weak or insecure may prevent emotionally immature individuals from utilizing their communication skills to ask for help, whether it be guidance from a coworker or acknowledging burnout at work.

- **Poor response to stress:** Emotional immaturity often manifests as difficulty in handling stress. Repressing emotions and failing to address them can lead to stress-related reactions such as increased anxiety, disrupted sleep patterns, and migraines. Reacting negatively to stress and allowing it to affect relationships with others may indicate emotional immaturity.

By recognizing these signs and understanding the areas where we need growth, we can actively work towards developing emotional maturity. It is a lifelong process that involves consistently engaging with our emotions, taking responsibility for our actions, seeking help when needed, and effectively managing stress. Through these efforts, we can cultivate emotional resilience and a deeper understanding of ourselves, leading to healthier relationships and a more fulfilling life.

Seeking External Guidance and Wisdom

In today's society, it has become more evident than ever that people need to prioritize their overall well-being, including physical, mental, and emotional health. As a result, holistic wellness retreats have become a popular and effective solution for individuals to achieve that balance. These retreats offer an immersive experience that incorporates various elements, such as mindfulness practices, nutritious food and cooking classes, fitness activities, spa therapies, and alternative healing practices. By addressing an individual's physical, mental, emotional, and spiritual needs, the retreat aims to provide a well-rounded and transformative experience.

During a holistic wellness retreat, participants have the opportunity to learn and practice mindfulness. Guided meditation sessions can help individuals relax and reduce anxiety, while yoga classes can improve physical flexibility and balance while also calming the mind. By incorporating these practices into daily life, individuals can better manage their stress levels.

Nutrition is also an essential element of a holistic wellness retreat. Many retreats offer organic, locally sourced, and nutrient-dense meals to support optimal health. Participants can attend cooking classes and workshops to learn about healthy eating habits. The focus is on mindful eating and developing an understanding of the relationship between food, energy, and well-being. By being present during meals and paying attention to hunger and satiety cues, individuals can develop a healthier relationship with food.

Physical activity and fitness are other critical aspects of a holistic wellness retreat. These retreats offer a variety of activities, including yoga, hiking, cycling, strength training, and water sports, which are tailored to different fitness levels to ensure everyone can participate.

Creating an Environment of Growth

Coping with loneliness can be difficult, but there are strategies you can employ to overcome it. One effective approach is to cultivate healthy relationships with people who bring you joy and support. This can be achieved by spending quality time with them and making an effort to engage in conversation with someone every day.

There are three main types of connections you can establish with others. Firstly, there are intimate connections, which consist of people who love and care for you such as family and close friends. Secondly, there are relational connections formed with individuals you interact with regularly and share common interests such as colleagues or people you encounter during your daily routine, like the barista who serves your morning coffee. Lastly, there are collective connections, which involve people who share a group membership or affiliation such as fellow voters or those who practice the same faith as you.

Take a moment to evaluate the presence of meaningful, long-term relationships in each of these three areas of connection. Reflect on whether you tend to stick with old friends and struggle to meet new people, or if you have an inclination to avoid individuals from your past and prefer the company of those who are not familiar with your personal history. It's important to be honest with yourself about your social habits.

Consider the type of relationships you currently have and the ones you desire. You might discover a desire to cultivate new friendships or seek to strengthen existing connections. One way to enhance your social bonds is by reaching out to people you already know, such as coworkers, family members, old school friends, or neighbors. Initiate a phone call, write an email, or send a message letting them know that you would like to stay in touch more frequently. Plan activities like meeting up for coffee, sharing a meal, enjoying music together, playing golf, or engaging in a game of chess. Identify the mutual interests that can serve as a foundation for these interactions. Additionally, leveraging social media platforms like Facebook can be a valuable tool for maintaining contact with others.

Essence of Self-Reflection

Self-reflection is a practice that allows us to delve beyond the surface level of our thoughts and emotions. It involves a deliberate and dedicated effort to turn our attention inward and explore our inner world. By examining our thoughts, emotions, and experiences, we gain a deeper understanding of who we are and what drives our actions.

Self-reflection is a transformative practice that involves exploring our inner world with curiosity and without judgment. When we engage in self-reflection, we take the time to observe our values and behaviors. We become curious about the patterns and dynamics that shape our lives, allowing us to gain valuable insights.

Through self-reflection, we start to notice recurring themes, habits, and reactions that may have gone unnoticed before. This heightened awareness helps us make conscious choices about how we want to live our lives. We can identify patterns that may be serving us well and reinforce them while also recognizing patterns that may be holding us back and working to change them.

Self-reflection is not a one-time activity; it is an ongoing practice that requires dedicated time and space for introspection. We must create an environment that allows us to quiet the noise of the external world and connect with our inner selves. This may involve finding moments of solitude, practicing mindfulness or meditation, journaling, or simply being alone with our thoughts. By creating this space, we can delve deep into our thoughts and emotions and gain a clearer understanding of ourselves.

Self-reflection also allows us to gain a profound awareness of our emotions and triggers. By developing this awareness, we can make conscious choices about how we respond to situations and challenges. We become better equipped to navigate life's ups and downs with clarity and wisdom.

Revisiting and Renewing Commitments

Life goals are much more than mere survival objectives or daily routines; they hold profound meaning and determine our long-term behaviors. While not strictly defined by psychology or clinical constructs, life goals help us identify what we truly desire to experience based on our values.

Given their nature, life goals can take on various forms. However, they provide us with a sense of direction and hold us accountable as we strive for happiness and overall well-being, working towards achieving our best lives.

There is often an emphasis on living in the present moment and being mindful. We are encouraged to avoid dwelling on the past or worrying about the future, as we aim to be the best version of ourselves in the present. However, amidst this focus on the present, we sometimes overlook the value of reflecting on our past experiences with love and appreciation.

While we should avoid getting stuck in the past and ruminating on it, taking the time to acknowledge where we've been and how far we've come can be a powerful practice. Reflecting on our past experiences can help us cultivate gratitude, recognize our growth and progress, and gain perspective on the journey we have been on.

By appreciating our past, we can understand the lessons we've learned, celebrate our achievements, and acknowledge the resilience that has brought us to where we are today. This reflection does not detract from living in the present; instead, it enhances our ability to fully embrace and appreciate the present moment.

"Remember how far you've come, not how far you have to go. You are not where you want to be, but neither are you where you used to be." -Rick Warren

I cannot emphasize how important emotional well-being is for teens. Each step in this book has brought you closer to mastering your emotions and getting a better understanding of yourself. While everyone is unique, there will be takeaways for everyone from this guide. Although this might be the end of the book, it is the beginning of a new journey for you. It's time to explore and see where your journey takes you.

CONCLUSION

This concludes our guide to emotional mastery for teens. It has been an amazing journey, and it's all about helping you on your journey towards better emotional control and well-being. Take your time and reflect on what this book has taught you. Whether it's labeling emotions or understanding your true self, this book has something for everyone.

Don't let this journey end here. Continue learning and moving ahead towards emotional mastery. Apply the techniques introduced in this book, and make sure you continue practicing them diligently. It's only a matter of time before you will master your emotions with ease and avoid getting overwhelmed with anxiety. If you feel this book helped you, help others as well. Leave a review and share your story with other like-minded teens. Don't let your learnings go to waste, and ensure all teens learn from your inspirational transformation.

REFERENCES

e. e. cummings Quotes. (n.d.). BrainyQuote.
  https://www.brainyquote.com/quotes/e_e_cummings_161593

*Miranda Otto Quote: "I think you go through a period as a teenager
  of being quite cool and unaffected by things."* (n.d.).
  Quotefancy.com. Retrieved October 3, 2023, from
  https://quotefancy.com/quote/1648817/Miranda-Otto-I-think-
  you-go-through-a-period-as-a-teenager-of-being-quite-
  cool-and

Brandy. (2018, March 15). *50 Mindfulness Quotes for Kids to Help
  Your Students Now*. The Counseling Teacher. https://thecoun-
  selingteacher.com/2018/03/50-mindfulness-quotes-to-help-
  your.html

Nguyen, R. (2018, May 11). *Don't Forget to Appreciate How Far You've
  Come*. Tiny Buddha. https://tinybuddha.com/blog/dont-forget-
  appreciate-how-far-youve-come/

Milton Keynes UK
Ingram Content Group UK Ltd.
UKHW010246221123
432980UK00005B/519

9 798989 429028